The PRODUCTIVITY HANDBOOK

*New Ways of Leveraging Your Time,
Information & Communications*

DONALD E. WETMORE

RANDOM HOUSE REFERENCE

NEW YORK   TORONTO   LONDON   SYDNEY   AUKLAND

Please address inquiries about electronic licensing of any products for use on a network, in software or on CD-ROM to the Subsidiary Rights Department, Random House Information Group, fax 212-572-6003.

This book is available for special discounts for bulk purchases for sales promotions or premiums. Special editions, including personalized covers, excerpts of existing books, and corporate imprints, can be created in large quantities for special needs. For more information, write to Random House, Inc., Special Markets/ Premium Sales, 1745 Broadway, MD 6-2, New York, NY, 10019 or e-mail specialmarkets@randomhouse.com.

Visit the Random House Reference Web site: www.randomwords.com

Library of Congress Cataloging-in-Publication Data is available.

First Edition

Printed in the United States of America

10 9 8 7 6 5 4 3 2 1

ISBN: 0-375-72114-2

THIS BOOK IS DEDICATED TO MY WIFE,
NANCY, AND OUR FOUR CHILDREN, JENNIFER,
PAMELA, CHRISTOPHER, AND JONATHAN, AS
PROOF POSITIVE THAT "ANY DREAM WILL DO."

Praise for *The Productivity Handbook*

Donald Wetmore has made a difference both to my private and professional life for which I am forever very grateful!
—Hans Barth, Vice President, Credit Suisse, Canada

Donald Wetmore has produced an outstanding, step-by-step guide for busy people to use to regain control of their lives and their schedules. He teaches you how to get more done in less time and how to avoid the pitfalls of letting other people and unexpected situations control your schedule. This is a "must read" for every busy individual, from corporate CEO to household executive!
—Ed Foreman, President, Executive Development Systems, Inc., Professional Speaker, Former Member of U.S. Congress

The Productivity Handbook is an outstanding resource.... It offers a step-by-step success formula for maximizing time to get more done in less time.
—Frederick K. Biebel, Former Deputy National Chairman of the Republican National Committee

For four consecutive years, Stew Leonard's has been named as one of Fortune magazine's "100 Best Companies to Work For." All our managers are required to take Don Wetmore's time management and productivity seminar. The Productivity Handbook *book will be required reading, too!*
—Stew Leonard, Jr. President & CEO, Stew Leonard's

Acknowledgments

This book became a reality because of the efforts of two talented professionals who patiently worked the concept to reality.

First, my thanks and gratitude go to my literary agent, John Willig of Literary Services, Inc., the consummate optimist and professional. His singular dedication husbanded this project from its inception with encouragement and constant attention to detail.

Second, my thanks and gratitude go to my editor, Jena Pincott of Random House. Her keen intellect, superb vision, and unparalleled editing skills helped transform a rough stone into a polished jewel.

Table of Contents

Part 3. Communication

Introduction

⟵━━◆━━⟶

This is not your father's productivity handbook.

Here, we take a fresh, new look at the timeless topic of time management as it needs to be practiced in the Information Age. Information is the currency of power, and you need to know how to manage it to maintain your competitive edge. The effective use of information is as important to your personal productivity as the traditional time management tools and techniques from the past.

Traditionally, time management was a topic restricted to the tools and techniques that help you squeeze more out of each day—gadgets, to-do lists, fancy calendar systems, and the like. *The Productivity Handbook* identifies a treasure trove of such tools—they're still necessary—but it also introduces a new way of looking at productivity. Productivity doesn't just mean doing more things *faster*. It means being more *effective* by living a balanced life.

In light of this, I developed what I call the productivity triangle, which encompasses time, information, and communication. At one base are traditional time management tools and techniques. At another are skills for increasing your ability to absorb information effectively. Add to this better communication skills. Combined, you have a formula for long-range personal planning skills as well as the foundation of physical, psychological, and emotional well-being. This is the way to gain better control and balance in your daily life. These are the real tools you need to maximize your personal productivity.

This concept is applied to the parts of *The Productivity Handbook*.

Part I, Time, offers you tools and techniques, including daily planning tips for managing multiple priorities, overcoming procrastination, effective delegation, managing interruptions, and maintaining personal balance while working against a set life plan of action, helping you to live your days with purpose rather than by accident.

Part II, Information, is designed to help you take in more of the right kind of information and do it more efficiently. It includes tips on how to shrink your inbox, write effective notes, improve your memory, and remember names.

Part III, Communication, reveals a wealth of tips to help you be a more effective communicator, which is crucial to your overall productivity. This part includes tips on how to maximize your connections and make new ones, lead more productive meetings, and be a better public speaker.

Obviously, these three parts are interdependent. You may be good at managing your time and absorbing information but not be as good at communicating your information. You may have strengths in absorbing and communicating information but be weak in managing your time. In today's world, it is not enough that you cover one or two bases of the productivity triangle. You have to practice and master all three.

Part IV, The Big Picture, brings together the tips and techniques learned in the previous chapters and helps you apply them to your values and your life goals.

The philosophy behind *The Productivity Handbook* is that time management must be put in the context of the big picture. It's not about how quickly you can accomplish something today, but how effectively you can leverage your time over the course of your lifetime. This is true productivity and the only real way to fulfill your dreams. Read this book as your first step toward achieving the goals you never thought you had time to accomplish. Use it at work and in life.

Most of all, enjoy your journey!

Donald E. Wetmore
Stratford, Connecticut

In this section, you will acquire tools and techniques to help you get more done in less time and with more balance in your life. Practice is the key to your success. Incorporate the suggestions offered in each chapter into your daily routine and watch your personal productivity soar.

PART **1** TIME

1

BALANCE

The Foundation of a Productive Life

⟶ ◆ ⟶

John didn't get his raise because his boss told him that his work always comes in late. But John has a good reason for his tardiness: *He never has enough time.* Today it was because he had to stop for gas on the way to work. He couldn't fill his tank yesterday because he was working too late and the gas station closed before he could get there. He was working late yesterday because he came in late to work that morning. He was running late that morning because he had to iron a shirt, and because of that, he didn't even have time to eat breakfast. He couldn't fill up the tank the night before, either. He had to make it to his after-work softball game, and on the way, he had to stop to put air in his leaky tire because he forgot to get it fixed last weekend. Last weekend was busy because he had to watch the game on Sunday. After all, the guys at work would all be talking about it on Monday and he did not want to feel left out. His colleagues' opinions of him are more important than his own.

Even though John has the tools and techniques to better control and manage his time, he doesn't use them because it is so much easier to drift and spend the day responding rather than taking the initiative. Anyway, what would the others say if he achieved more than they did?

John believes that people succeed when they get lucky breaks. They hit it just at the right time, while John, without having bad luck, would have no luck at all.

John believes that's true for himself and for his family and always has been and always will be. We cannot change who we are or where we came from or the bad fortune that is our fate. We have to learn to accept what life gives to us and ask for no more.

So, John went home that night without his raise and promotion. It was just as he expected.

THE REAL MEANING OF PRODUCTIVITY

If you ask most people what comes to mind when they think about time management and personal productivity, you will typically get answers that refer to the *tools* of time management: to-do lists, notepads, and PDAs (personal digital assistants such as Palm handhelds and BlackBerries). These are useful and essential tools for enhancing your productivity (and will be discussed in this book), but they themselves are secondary to a more fundamental requirement: a balanced life built on a sturdy foundation. As in John's case, small problems can lead to major breakdowns. Any house built on a weak foundation is destined to collapse, and so will a life if it isn't balanced. The foundation of your life consists of seven areas:

1. *Health*
2. *Family*
3. *Financial*
4. *Intellectual*
5. *Social*
6. *Professional*
7. *Spiritual*

You may not spend the same amount of time in each area or time every day in each area, but if you do over the long run, then your life will be in balance and your foundation will be sound.

My point about the relationship between productivity and life balance is best explained by describing what happens if you *don't* have balance. Take health, for example. With the stresses of daily life, let's say you are not getting a sufficient quantity or quality of sleep. Tired people have no energy. They have trouble thinking, speaking, and making decisions. Tests reveal that tired people have difficulty remembering things and tend to feel more emotional and unstable. They may also be impatient, antisocial, and unimaginative.

In fact, there's a good chance that you're tired right now even as you read this page. Three out of four of us are just flat-out tired all the time. Go up to ten strangers, at any time of the day, and ask them, "Are you rested?" "Did you get a good night's sleep?" "Are you a bundle of energy today?" Three out of four people will tell you how tired they are.

Many people are tired because they stay up too late to provide enough time for their bodies to get sufficiently recharged. Others do not get the quality of sleep they need. They are filled with lots of stress and feeling out of control because they do not have the tools or refuse to use tools to take more control over their time each day.

Your fatigue will affect all seven areas of your life, starting with your family, social life, and professional life. It may also affect your capacity to be financially secure, intellectually fulfilled, and spiritually sound. In other words, a deficit in one area can and does affect every aspect of your life.

A deficit in one area can and does affect every aspect of your life.

←——◆◆——→

You can load up lots of tools into your time management toolbox. You can have the best new gadgets, the tidiest to-do lists, and the best intentions, but if you are too tired to access these tools, they do you no good.

And your health is just one of seven areas that, if neglected, can throw your entire life (and productivity) off balance.

THE SEVEN AREAS OF A BALANCED LIFE

For a truly productive life, you need to keep the following in balance.

Health

The health category covers your physical health—how rested, fit, and vigorous you are.

As I mentioned above, health is the area that we tend to value the least until we don't have it anymore. Some 2.4 million people will die in the United States this year, 75 percent of whom will die prematurely. For example, the number-one killer is heart disease. More than one in three of us will die of that one cause alone. Some of the causes of heart problems are hereditary and environmental, but most are within our control. Diet, weight, exercise, and stress can be controlled. But it takes a commitment.

We all have the best intentions to stay healthy by getting

more sleep and exercising. But 90 percent of the people who sign up for health clubs today will stop going in the next ninety days. We start off by going two or three times each week and then something comes along so we skip a week and then it's two weeks and then we are out of the loop entirely.

Neglecting your health may cost you time to correct the damage you have created. A friend of mine had back surgery a few years ago and at the conclusion of her treatment her surgeon advised her to conduct a daily routine of simple calisthenics and stretches to prevent a recurrence of her back problem. Not a major task, perhaps ten minutes a day.

Unfortunately, she could never find the time to follow this simple but important prescription and now she spends about twelve hours a week going to physical therapy to undo a problem she created.

The bottom line, as it relates to health and productivity, is that you have to take time for health and fitness today or you will have to take time for sickness and illness tomorrow. If time management means anything, it means making choices every day that add a few extra years at the end of your life, giving you more time to manage.

Family

The family category covers your immediate family of husband, wife, significant other, children, parents, and so on and your extended family of cousins, aunts, uncles, and close friends.

Few need to be convinced about the importance of spending time, quality time, with family and extended family. For many, the events of September 11, 2001, brought that issue closer to home.

This year there will be approximately 2 million marriages in the United States. That is so nice! And there will be approximately 1 million divorces. How sad. And what a waste of time! The years of upset over a bad relationship will waste more time than you think. The emotional and financial implications of a crumbling relationship can set you back for years.

The primary cause of divorce is a lack of communication. The average working person spends less than two minutes a day in meaningful communication with his or her spouse or significant other and less than thirty seconds each day in meaningful communication with his or her children. And we wonder why 50 percent of the marriages are going down the drain.

Now, when couples begin their relationship, they spend time together. They go places together and they laugh and cry together. Then the relationship is confirmed and stuff comes along that keeps them apart. He travels here and she works nights and like two ships in the dark they pass each other and eventually lose sight of each other.

A sales manager asked me once, "With my busy schedule, how do I take my four year old on vacation this year?" I thought for a moment and replied, "You take her when she's four years old." Likewise, there is only one way to tell your seventy-year-old mother that you love her. You have to tell her when she's seventy years old. Sometimes, the most obvious answer eludes us. Take the time—*now.*

Financial

The financial category covers your financial health and money-related goals.

Each of us spends, on average, 50 percent of our waking hours making a living. The average American works around forty-five hours a week and spends another couple of hours each day for preparation and commuting time. In total, the average American spends about fifty-five hours a week, or about half his or her available time, making a living.

Earnings levels in this world range anywhere from zero (do nothing and get nothing) to the billion-dollar salaries of

> **The emotional and financial implications of a crumbling relationship can set you back for years.**
>
> ←—•—→

Bill Gates and Oprah Winfrey. I don't know much about these people beyond what I read in the media. They seem to be talented, but the notion that they are billions of times more talented than the average person is not realistic. Do they have more time than the average person? No, of course not. They have the same amount of time as all of us. The answer? They achieve billions times more than the average person because they *use their time differently.*

The difference between those who are wildly wealthy and those who are not is that successful people take time away from their expense column and allocate it to their investment column. In other words, they use the time they have better and therefore earn more per working hour. Highly productive achievers leave their televisions off and spend that same time pursuing further education, sharpening their communication skills, and other activities that will produce more income over their work life and afford them more rewards during their lifetime.

—————————— *Intellectual* ——————————

The intellectual area covers the knowledge that you acquire and apply toward your life and, in particular, your career.

Some experts suggest that half of all human knowledge was unknown to us twenty years ago. The amount of information has doubled during the last twenty years from the beginning of time and is doubling even faster as we move forward. *Each day* some 50,000 volumes of information are being added to the Internet. That's the equivalent of a good-sized municipal library. How do you keep up?

The sharp increase in information affects your career most of all. Not too many years ago the rule was that you came into this world as a young person, and you learned a skill, trade, or profession. That knowledge base served you for a working lifetime of forty-plus years. Sure, you would improve as time went on, but you drew substantially from that skill set acquired early on in your life.

Today, for most of us, if we continue doing what we do in our various occupations without any improvement over the next several years, we face the real prospect of obsolescence. You may be the best (and most productive) designer of buggy whips, but if the world doesn't need buggy whips, you're out of work. Your competition, especially in business, is advancing all the time. Not only are young people graduating from college with fresh skills that are sometimes

> **Your success five years from now depends on what you are doing this week and month to upgrade your skills and polish your talents.**
>
> ←—◆◆—→

valued more than those acquired over a lifetime, but also your competitors may have been increasing their knowledge in ways you haven't.

You may be productive now, but you need to invest time in your education to be productive over the course of your entire life. Your success five years from now depends on what you are doing this week and month to upgrade your skills and polish your talents. Don't focus only on how you can be productive today in this moment, but how you can accomplish your goals over a lifetime.

———————————— *Social* ————————————

The social category covers all of your relationships with friends, colleagues, and people you meet. We all value these social relationships; without them we would live as hermits.

Besides the emotional benefits of having friends, the help of other people can save you enormous amounts of time, getting you answers, making introductions, or giving you advice that would take you forever to gather. I am not suggesting that those who do not have the cooperation of other people cannot be productive. Of course they can. They just cannot be *as* productive.

And the sad thing about this is that the people who haven't developed their social skills will never know what they missed. They will never know the invitations they did not receive or the networking opportunities that were never offered to them. They will never know the words of encouragement and pats on the back that could have pushed them forward at a time when they were stalled.

Professional

The professional category covers job satisfaction and career ambition.

Imagine having a new job starting tomorrow. The job is to sit at a desk for eight or nine hours straight and stare at a wall. You are not allowed to work on the computer, talk on the phone, or read a book. You just have sit there hour after hour. Now, you would receive the same paycheck on payday and have the same benefits. Would you take it?

My guess is you wouldn't. What would be missing in this easy but meaningless job is that internal satisfaction that comes to you from having done a good job, having made a difference in the world. Independent of the financial com-

> **The help of other people can save you enormous amounts of time, getting you answers, making introductions, or giving you advice that would take you forever to gather.**

pensation, we all need to feel like we are putting some footprints in the sand, that our actions have made a difference. This is crucial to a balanced life. Why be productive in a career that you don't find fulfilling? (Chances are you won't be anyway.)

A fulfilling career doesn't have to be a traditional office job. For many years, my wife, Nancy, was a full-time housewife working each day to raise our four children and run our household. Nancy did not receive a salary for her work, but she went to bed each night knowing that she had made a lot of difference in many people's lives.

Spiritual

The spiritual category covers the tools you have to cope with and transcend everyday problems.

While I do not advocate any particular religious philosophy or creed, I know most of us practice a faith in one of many ways, from organized religion to forms of yoga. But beyond the issue of religion, when I refer to the spiritual area, I also refer to your outlook on life.

Through the years, I have met so many people who have said to me, "Show me how to get rid of my current set of problems and my life will be just perfect!" I always respond with the truth: When you retire your current set of problems, you have another fresh set coming right at you. Life is a constant series of problems. You are never without problems.

Productivity does not require you to rid your life of problems, but it does require you to handle your problems better. Your spirituality will help you to achieve this balance and maintain an outlook on life that will empower you to do more things. The time you invest in spiritual pursuits or meditation will help you in the other areas of your life. Without that center, you may find yourself struggling.

Throughout the rest of this book, keep in mind these seven areas of a balanced life for if they are not in balance, none of the tips and techniques here will be effective over the long term.

Put another way, productivity is the art, science, and practice of taking better control of the twenty-four hours of each day in a way that fosters balance and harmony. If you don't

> **If you don't consciously balance your life, someone, or lots of someones and somethings, will gladly step up and take control of it for you.**

consciously balance your life, someone, or lots of someones and somethings, will gladly step up and take control of it for you. Your family will clamor for all your attention. Your financial ambitions may eat up all your time. You might spend all day and night building your career. Likewise, a busy social life might deplete the other six areas of your life. In the long run, your overall productivity diminishes. It might even reach a point where you can't even continue what you have been doing because of a crisis in another area. You can't let that happen.

2

THE BIG TO-DO

The Importance of Daily Planning

In one famous chapter of Lewis Carroll's *Alice in Wonderland,* Alice comes to a fork in the road. Unfamiliar with the territory, she turns to a big smiling Cheshire cat for directions, "Do I go left or right?"

The cat in turn asks Alice a poignant question, "Where are you going?"

Alice replies, "I don't know."

The cat retorts, "Well, then take either road."

If you don't know where you are going, you will never know when you get there. What difference does it make which road you are on?

I do not believe there is any intrinsic reward in being a manager, a CEO, a parent, or anything else for that matter unless you know where you are going and whether or not that path is taking you to where you want to go. You can be the world's most productive person, but it doesn't matter unless your efforts are directed toward a goal.

You walk around every day with a book under your arm. Let's call it your *Book of Life*. It has seven chapters in it, one for each of the seven areas of your life: health, family, financial, intellectual, social, professional, and spiritual. Every day you live is a new page.

How do you want the book to end? What will it say about you and your life? What will it say about your family? How far will you have gone in your career? Were you in good health and spirits for much of your life? Will there be a happy ending?

Why focus on the last day of your life? Because that is the *only* day in your life when you cannot change the way the story ends. Until then, it does not matter what may be broken or damaged in your life. Whether you have financial struggles, professional difficulties, or relationship issues, you have the opportunity to change your future. How? By working backward to figure out what you have to do each day to get to where you want to go.

I like to use the example of former President Bill Clinton to illustrate the point. Thirty years before Clinton became president of the United States, he was a member of a youth group called Boys Nation. On a trip to Washington, D.C., he and his friends toured historical sites and met President John F. Kennedy in the Rose Garden at the White House. (In fact, there is a famous photograph of young Clinton shaking hands with President Kennedy in the garden.) Clinton says that this was the moment when he decided to become president.

Of course, Clinton did not go from teenager to president overnight. It was a long path with many steps along the way. The difference between the very successful and the less successful is not that the successful people are moving faster on the path; rather, they are traveling with foresight. (The purpose of this book is not to show you how to go faster because that just burns you out a lot faster.)

Clinton went through many little steps to achieve his big goal. First, he was the governor of Arkansas for several years. To be the governor, he first served as the attorney general for the state of Arkansas. To be the attorney general, he worked as a law professor. To be a law professor, he had to go to law school and pass the bar exam. To get into the right law school, he had to do well in college. To get into the right college, he had to do well in high school. And to do

> **You can be the world's most productive person, but it doesn't matter unless your efforts are directed toward a goal.**

well in high school, he had to do a good job on his history exam on Wednesday.

See it? That's the little step in this journey of a thousand miles. When you identify where you want to go in any area of your life and work your way backward to identify the steps, you will always find that the next step is within your reach. Suddenly, your goal is realizable.

Clinton wasn't born with the financial resources that would guarantee success. Surely, he encountered people who laughed at him. But he had the discipline and the foresight to ignore the skeptics, study hard, and plan ahead. He must have known that becoming president of the United States starts with, say, acing freshman history.

The lesson here for you is that when you have done the hard work of determining where you truly want to go in your life, you need to work your way backward to figure out what you need to do this year, this month, this week, and this day. When you break your goals down into steps, you'll see that it becomes easier to decide exactly how to spend your time.

The best way to do this is to have a *daily plan*.

YOUR DAILY PLAN

An old expression comes to mind: "If you want to get something done, give it to a busy person." True, isn't it? You've probably noticed how productive you become the day before you leave for a two-week vacation. You become a fire-ball of activity because you have to get those things done before going away. The good news is you do not need to go on vacation to give you that same sense of urgency. You can create that same environment each day by building a great to-do list each night, drawing on your inventory of "have tos" and "want tos."

Here's how to do it.

1. Start a Daily To-Do List

If you want to manage it, you have to measure it. First, get a pad of paper or your PDA and start your list. Visit your local stationery supply store to review a variety of options. You could use a regular notepad. I use a Day-Timer paper system sold by the Day-Timer Company in Allentown, Pennsylvania. A Palm handheld or BlackBerry is a great choice as well. The only requirement is that your daily plan-

> **When you identify where you want to go in any area of your life and work your way backward to identify the steps, you will always find that the next step is within your reach.**

ner must be simple and user-friendly. Make sure your choice is light and compact.

Now, there are two dimensions to daily planning. First, appointments and scheduled events. These are time-sensitive commitments to be at a certain place at a certain time. For example, a sales meeting on Tuesday, 3:00 P.M., Aunt Susan's birthday party on Sunday, 5:00 P.M., and the dentist on Saturday, 9:00 A.M.

All the rest of your time, beyond that allocated for appointments and scheduled events, is called discretionary time. It is time to work, at your discretion, on your want tos and have tos that you have built into your action lists.

In your daily planner, create an inventory of all the things you have to do and a list of all the things you want to do.

Here is what a have-to-do list might look like:

Call Tom
Back up computer
Ryder research project
Call Susan
Budget
Review contract
Client calls
Create marketing brochure

Here's what a want-to-do list might look like:

Read sales training manual
Call Grandma
Plan family vacation
Write thank-you note to sister
Help Billy with his homework
Sign up to coach Mary's team
Take clothes to Goodwill
Brush the dog

For practical purposes, combine the two lists into one to-do list. Most people will have started with a list of have-to items that is fairly long and a list of want-to items that is much longer. But here is the good news. As you build in more and more items to your list of things to do each day, you will take advantage of Parkinson's Law, which states, in part, that a project tends to expand with the time allocated for it. If you give yourself one thing to do today, it will take

If you give yourself a dozen things to do today, you may not get twelve done, but you'll get nine done because having a lot to do automatically makes you a better time manager.

you all day to do it. If you give yourself two things to do today, you'll get both done. If you give yourself a dozen things to do today, you may not get twelve done, but you'll get nine done because having a lot to do automatically makes you a better time manager.

2. Determine How Many Items You Can Accomplish in One Day

I like to use a simple formula to determine how many items I can hope to accomplish in each day. I start with the total number of hours for tomorrow's workday, exclusive of lunch and breaks. Let's say tomorrow I will be spending a net of eight hours. From this I want to subtract time already committed for appointments and scheduled events. To-morrow, I have a sales meeting and a client appointment and combined, they will take two hours. I am now left with six hours.

Next, I want to factor in interruptions. I don't know when they will occur; that's what makes them interruptions. But knowing they will occur means I will not have all those six hours to work on my action list. Let's say I typically get two hours of interruptions in my day. Subtracting from six available hours, I'm down to four hours for my to-do list.

I like to overplan my day a bit because it gives me a healthy sense of pressure and urgency to get more focused, to get more done. I do not want, however, to overplan the day by so much that I accomplish only a tiny portion of what I planned to accomplish, leaving me feeling demoralized over the things I did not get done.

I overplan my days by a factor of 50 percent. By giving myself 50 percent more than I know I can reasonably handle, I create a positive sense of pressure but not to a point where it is overwhelming and self-defeating. With four available hours as calculated earlier and adding on 50 percent more for overplanning, I would build a to-do list for tomorrow that contains approximately six hours of action items.

3. Prioritize

Take a look at your to-do list. Some of the items are crucial with a high payback to your productivity, while other items are not crucial. When faced with choices between working on crucial or not-crucial items, many people will wind up working on the not-crucial items. Why? The crucial items are typically longer and more involved to complete. Not-crucial items are quick and more fun.

For example, perhaps the most crucial item on my list is to work on the Ryder research project. It is long and involved. On the other hand, there's a stack of junk mail that I would like to go through. My temptation is to do the junk mail. This may have some productive benefit but at the expense of a better use of my time.

You need a system that helps you focus on the crucial items on your list. I use an A, B, C, and D prioritizing system and mark items with an asterisk if they can be done in fewer than five minutes. (PDA users can also prioritize items on their list by inputting A, B, C, D, or * before each entry or using the prioritizing system that comes with the handheld.)

A = *Crucial*
B = *Important*
C = *Little value*
D = *No value*
* = *Quick item that can be done in less than five minutes*

My to-do list now looks like this:

B *Call Tom*
* *Back up computer*
A *Ryder research project*
B *Call Susan*
A *Budget*
B *Review contract*
A *Client calls*
D *Create marketing brochure*
C *Junk mail*
A *Write letters*
* *Filing*

A—This is for your crucial items, the things that will produce the highest productive payback to you. You have prioritized these items in light of your commitments and responsibilities to others and in consideration of your long-term goals and the balance you want in your life.

B—This is for the important items, the things that are productive but do not have that higher A value.

C—Represents the items of little value. Chances are you will not get to your C items on your list, but that's just fine because everything else you do will have a higher value. What is a C today will likely increase in importance to a B or A at a later date and get done.

D—These items have little urgency at the moment.

*—Label the "quickie" items on your list with an asterisk and complete them first in your day. Completing them will give your day a jumpstart. For example, "back up computer," which gets an asterisk, is an important but quick item. All I have to do is plug in my Zip drive to the laptop and click the mouse once or twice. The process just takes a few minutes. I typically have a few asterisk items on my list each day.

Can all items on your list be As? Theoretically, I suppose they can, but on a practical level, probably not. What if you discover you have no As on your list? You better get some; Otherwise you are working on low-priority items that produce, by definition, low levels of productivity.

Doing more of the crucial items in your day elevates your self-esteem. You feel better about yourself when you're taking on and accomplishing these crucial items. The reverse applies as well. When you get bogged down in the not-crucial items, your self-esteem can be diminished.

4. Subprioritize

Step 4, subprioritizing is optional, but it helps me and many of my clients. Imagine you are outdoors in the parking lot holding twenty pads of paper and a magnifying glass. Your task is to concentrate the sun's rays on the pads of paper and burn them all up. You start with the first pad. The concentrated rays from your magnifying glass burn through that pad. Good! Now you move over to the second pad to ignite it and while that happens, the flame on the first pad goes out. So you redirect the magnified rays to the first pad, get it going again, but then the second pad goes out. You move to the third pad, because, after all, you want to get them all done, and the first two go out.

Now at the end of the day, what have you got? You still have twenty pads of paper with several burn marks on each but you have not completely burned up one pad.

To apply the pad and magnifying lens principle to your to-do list, your goal is to "burn up" each item before moving on to the next. After all, you can't possibly work on all your A items simultaneously. This requires you to specify in what order you can accomplish things.

You can subprioritize the items on your list using the numeric system. I have four As on my sample list below. I cannot do them all at the same time, but I can do them one at a time. If I could work only on one item, which one would it be? In my judgment, it would be the Ryder research project. That item becomes my A-1. Then if there is time, the second item I will address is letters. That becomes my A-2. Then I will work on budget, my A-3. My A-4 will be client calls. I will do the same for my B and C items. (If you are using a PDA, you can subprioritize the items by either sorting them in the preferred order or subprioritizing by typing in A, B, C, or D followed by the number as you would on paper.)

The completed prioritized action list now looks like this:

B-3 *Call Tom*
* *Back up computer*
A-1 *Ryder research project*
B-2 *Call Susan*
A-3 *Budget*
B-4 *Review contract*
A-4 *Client calls*
D-1 *Create marketing brochure*
C-1 *Junk mail*
A-2 *Write letters*
* *Filing*

What you have accomplished here is a list of action items for the next day, prioritized in the order of their importance. When you go to bed each night, you'll sleep better because you'll have a sense of certainty and control about your next day. The following morning you'll work on the asterisk items first. Then you'll tackle the items in the order of their importance, maybe not getting everything done, but almost certainly getting the most important items done.

YOUR MONTHLY CALENDAR

The other task of daily planning is to plan out appointments and scheduled events, specific time-sensitive commitments, weeks and even months in advance. I like to use a month-at-a-glance calendar. Your daily planner or PDA will probably include this type of calendar.

The ability to see each day of the months ahead gives you the benefits of context, anticipation, and integration. Ask yourself these three questions before you make commitments:

- *What else is going on?* Before you schedule an appointment or event, consider when it falls in relation to your other commitments. For example, a client calls today and asks if I am free to meet on the 30th of the month at 2:00 P.M. at her office some forty-five minutes from my office. I look at my month-at-a-glance calendar and see that the space is available. I would be inclined to schedule this appointment as requested. But before I do, I flip the page on my calendar to the next month and note that I have an appointment with another client in the same city one week later. It makes good sense to combine both engagements, so I will suggest the alternate date to my client. Ninety-five percent of the time, when someone is asking of your time, there is an alternative date and time that will work just as well. By combining these two appointments, I just saved an hour and a half of extra travel time.

This may not work every time. My client may insist on a meeting on the 30th. If that is the case, my next phone call is to the person I am scheduled to visit one week later and ask if he or she can move our time together one week earlier.

Another example: A client asks for a meeting on a Friday at 2:00 P.M. and I do not have another commitment anytime soon in his area, but I see that on the following day, Saturday, my family and I are off on a two-week vacation. I don't know about you, but the day before I'm going away on vacation, my focus is not 100 percent on business. So in the context of my personal schedule, it would be more productive to schedule that important business meeting at a more appropriate and productive time.

- *Are you a racehorse or a tortoise?* A racehorse thrives on overload. That's what gets its juices flowing. A tortoise likes to handle things at a slower, more measured pace. If I have to set five different appointments for next week and I am a racehorse, I would try to set up three for Monday and two for Tuesday, for example, overloading my days. A tortoise might set one appointment for each of the five workdays. At the end of the week, both the racehorse and the tortoise have accomplished the same number of appointments. They have just done it differently.

- *Are you a morning bird or night owl?* Some of us are morning people, meaning that we experience our highest energy levels earlier rather than later in the day. There are also night people, who experience their highest energy levels later in the day. (And some of us are just no darn good any time of the day!) Determine where you fit in and schedule yourself accordingly. A morning person would want to schedule high-level, important commitments for earlier in the day, where possible, whereas the night person would opt for later in the day. Just go with the flow by assessing who you are and leveraging it to your advantage.

POOR PLANNING

←———◆———→

A student in one of my seminars told me he lost out on a $10,000 deal in just one day. He was a computer analyst for a local company. He also did computer-consulting work on the side. In addition, he was the coach for the kids' soccer team. In other words, he had several balls in the air.

One day he received a call from one of his consulting clients, a client who provided him with about $10,000 in consulting fees each year. The client asked if he would be available to do some consulting work on Thursday the 15th of the month at 8:00 P.M. He looked at his consulting calendar, saw nothing on the 15th, and said, "Sure." Unfortunately, he didn't look at his other two calendars, the ones for his personal life and his corporate job. As it turns out, the 15th was also the day that his boss, the executive vice president, was coming to the office from across the country for his semiannual visit. It was also the day of his son's championship soccer game.

My student went to work that day and was dragged through an exhausting routine. At 5:00 he tried to leave to coach the kids, but the boss was still there. Finally, at about 5:15 P.M., he absolutely had to leave, which angered and insulted his boss, who had flown 3,000 miles to be there.

My student rushed home, changed clothes for the soccer game, and dashed across town to the soccer field. He arrived late and frustrated and the kids were all over the field, no organization, not practicing, just fooling around. He went off on a tirade about their lack of self-control and discipline and said some things he wished he had not said. His words sunk their morale so low that they lost the game and the league championship.

Then he left the soccer game, rushed home, took a shower, and changed his clothes again, but was still forty minutes late for his consulting job and even more stressed and frustrated. The client, angered at having to wait, terminated the relationship. At the end of that day, my student damaged his career and his relationship with his boss, caused his son's team to lose their game, and lost his lucrative consulting job—all because he didn't effectively schedule his day.

You should be able to go to one calendar that has all of your appointments and scheduled events, both business and personal, and review each upcoming scheduled commitment and ask yourself, "What can I do in anticipation of this event coming up tomorrow [next week, next month]?" I have my annual physical scheduled for later this month. Perhaps I should make up a list of questions to ask the doctor to make our time together more productive. I'm going to a staff meeting on Tuesday. How about if I write up an agenda to make that meeting more productive? These specific improvements should be added to your to-do list on the day you think you might be able to act on them.

YOUR NIGHTLY COMMITMENT

Set aside some time each evening, if possible, for daily planning—preparing your to-do lists and looking over your monthly calendar.

Reviewing your schedule and to-do list at night permits you to prioritize your life's goals and commitments. A side benefit of this is that when you go to bed each night, you'll sleep with a sense of certainty and control that you otherwise wouldn't enjoy. I swear that the quality of your sleep will be enhanced when tomorrow's action items are listed on your to-do lists and calendar and not in your head. For some, daily planning may be impractical because of many other responsibilities. If that's true for you, do it first thing in the morning. The most important point is, *do your daily planning before you start your day.*

3

THE HORSE'S SECRET

GETTING AN EDGE IN YOUR DAILY ROUTINE

❦

A horse race has a first-place winner and a runner-up. Often, the first-place horse earns twice the prize as the second-place horse. Curiously, the number-one horse does not have to run twice as fast or go twice as far as the number-two horse for its owner to win twice the money. It only has to be a nose ahead when it crosses the finish line.

Time management, productivity, and success in life are in some ways like a horse race. To get twice as much in life in any one of your seven areas (health, family, financial, intellectual, social, professional, and spiritual), you do not have to double your efforts. You only need to do what you do just a little bit better to get a nose ahead of where you are now. Never underestimate the power of slight, painless modifications.

SMALL CHANGES FOR BIG RESULTS

Small changes in your daily routine yield huge dividends. The following exercises are guaranteed to give you the edge you seek. Use them to be more effective over the long term.

1. Carry Your A-1 Priorities with You All the Time

Take a look at all the A-1 priority items you wrote down on your daily to-do list. Do you really need to be at your desk to accomplish them?

Always have stuff with you that you can work on. Perhaps a work project or two, some business reading, your laptop, or the envelopes for your Christmas card list. If you get delayed, you have the option of making use of what could be wasted time.

After all, we all encounter delays. Face it: You will be delayed in traffic, at the dentist, in an airport, or in a line at the bank or elsewhere. There is little you can do about it. Going crazy or being unhappy will not make the delay shorter.

I was recently on a flight to San Francisco from Newark, New Jersey. The plane pushed back from the gate and suddenly stopped. The pilot announced that we had lost our clearance because of an impending thunderstorm. We returned to the gate, where we were informed that no one could leave the plane. At times such as this, it never ceases to amaze me how groups react. About 20 percent—one in five—fomented into an angry mob that tormented the flight attendants with questions such as, "How *dare* they cancel this flight? This is the fifth time this has happened." About 60 percent became the passive plenty who just sat and did nothing, took it all in, and murmured, "Okay. We're not going to fly. Okay." The remaining 20 percent were the productive pool, the people who know delays are inevitable. They prepared accordingly and had an A-1, high-priority project or two with them to convert the delay into productive time.

I like to belong to the third group. I pulled out my call folder and was able to get caught up on my phone messages. I had my laptop with me and wrote two articles. I had my budget spreadsheets and was able to do some advanced planning.

Some other ideas for making use of delays:

- *Bring your telephone contact list.* Think ahead of where you are going and ask yourself what telephone numbers would be useful if you were delayed. Friends? Family? Business associates? Your travel agent? Make sure you have these telephone numbers with you so that when you get delayed, if you have access to a telephone, you give yourself more choices to be productive.

- *Bring some entertainment.* What do you like? Are you into crossword puzzles? Crafts? Game Boy? If you are prepared for it, delay time can be down time.
- *Sit and think.* In our hurry-up world we have little time just to think about our lives, where we have been, where we are now, and where we are going. Use delay time to reflect on your life and celebrate the good things that are happening and commit to changing what needs to be improved.

2. 7 x 7 Exponential Improvements

At the customer service desk or the exit of some stores, you will often notice a customer suggestion box. Some retailers actually take the suggestions seriously. One good example is a client of mine, Stew Leonard's, a large grocery store that specializes in dairy products. Each night all three boxes are emptied and all suggestions are reviewed. Some comments are not too helpful: "Give the food away for free, please." However, a fair percentage of the ideas are really neat. For example, they have a fresh

Always have stuff with you that you can work on.

←——•—→

fish counter and a produce counter at different places in the store. Customers who buy fresh fish often like fresh lemons to go along with their fish but may forget to visit the produce department. So a customer suggested that they offer lemons for sale at the fish counter as well as at the produce department. Simple idea. A new lemon display was built for the fish counter and lemon sales dramatically increased.

Now imagine that you are the president of Me, Inc., a major corporation. You have some "sales" and "expenses" and you want to enjoy a profit every year. How about if you have your own customer suggestion box for daily job improvement? You're your own best customer (and your own best critic). Analyze your own job performance in the seven areas of your life and think of ways to improve each one slightly.

Each night in daily planning, besides putting down all the things you have to do to achieve your goals and the specific action steps required, take a moment to build in these little improvements. These are little things, but, at least until they become second nature to you, jot them down to remind yourself to do them. (Put an asterisk to the left of the entry to denote it as a "quickie" item that can be done in less than five minutes.) Here are a few examples in each category.

Health

You usually park your car close to the door. Tomorrow, for extra exercise, you make a point to park on the other side of the parking lot and walk a bit farther You usually take the elevator to the third floor. Tomorrow, you walk up the stairs. You usually eat dessert after dinner. Tomorrow, you skip the dessert.

Family

Tomorrow, leave a little love note under the pillow or in the briefcase of a loved one. My son used to take his lunch to school. In the morning while he was brushing his teeth, I would write him a quick note (Roses are red, Violets are blue. You're terrific, but so am I too! Love, Dad) and I would stick it under his peanut butter and jelly sandwich. At lunchtime, he would shake the contents out of his bag and, to his embarrassment, that note would appear in front of his friends. (He loved it, really.)

Here's another example: My wife's parents do not get to see their grandchildren as often as they would like because they live in another state. We take many pictures in our family, so when I get the processed photos back from the photo lab, I make it a point to send the in-laws a few of the snapshots. No letter, I just label the pictures, put them in an envelope, and mail them. How long does that take? A minute? The minute pays off in a big way by bringing my geographically distant family closer together.

—————————— *Professional* ——————————

Tomorrow, clean your office. Talk to someone in a different department and make a new connection. Figure out a new shortcut on your computer. Think of any small changes you can make in your career. Ask your colleagues and boss for feedback about your performance.

—————————— *Financial* ——————————

Tomorrow, brown bag your lunch and sock away the expense. If you save $10 each day where it can earn 5 percent interest, compounded, you will have $590,384 in forty-five years. I know, it's a long way away, but it's also a lot of money. Perhaps you might also like to set up an appointment with a financial planner or pick up a book on investing at the bookstore on your way home.

—————————— *Intellectual* ——————————

Tomorrow, expand your vocabulary by learning a new word, and continue the act of learning a new word the next day, and so on, for the rest of your life. A free service, A.Word.A.Day, makes this easy. To subscribe, go to www.wordsmith.org. Read fifteen minutes a day. Cut out fifteen minutes from your lunch hour. Get up fifteen minutes earlier or go to bed fifteen minutes later. Start watching television fifteen minutes later each evening. Leave twenty-three and three-quarter hours in your day as they are and just carve out fifteen minutes to read the books that are not getting read. Over the next ten years you will read an additional 120 books. (See chapter 10 on speed reading for additional tips on reading faster.)

Social

Tomorrow, send a cute greeting card to an old friend you haven't spoken to in some time. Compliment others. Almost every day I will go out of my way to genuinely and sincerely compliment someone on something that I perceive to be of value that he or she has done.

The other important one here is to remember birthdays and anniversaries. I have a list of all-important dates, some twenty-five or so, on a single sheet, listed in chronological order. I paper clip the list into my daily planner. If you have

> **One improvement a day multiplied by 7 days a week equals 49 improvements each week, equaling nearly 2,500 little improvements over the next year.**
>
> ←—•◆•—→

a PDA, you can simply type the dates in. I note the next date, and whatever I intend to do to celebrate that date—call the person, send a card, or buy a present. Put those action steps into the to-do list on the day you intend to do those things.

—————————— *Spiritual* ——————————

Tomorrow, take a moment for meditation or a minute of gratitude. I do this every night. As I drift off to sleep I go through each of the seven areas (health, family, financial, intellectual, social, professional, and spiritual) and rate my performance for the day on a scale of 1 to 10, with 10 being the highest, and then total up the score to see what a great day I had. I then thank God for the opportunity to live this day and I ask for one more. (If you think you are ever having some bad days, try missing a few.)

3. Manage Your Mornings

During the first fifteen or twenty minutes of your waking day, did you ever notice how you are awake but not fully awake? You are putting one foot in front of the other, but you are not 100 percent alert. It is during this time frame that you are in what is known as the alpha state. You are awake, conscious, but not at that fully awake state known as the beta state. In alpha, your brain waves and physical cycles are slowed and it is then that you are at the highest level of learning receptivity. Studies show that while in the alpha state, you can as much as double your learning rate because your brain waves and physical cycles are slowed and are conducive to learning. Young children are often in the alpha state.

Now why is this so important? Because in the alpha state you are at the highest level of learning receptivity. Many people, not understanding how this works, get up first thing in the morning and turn on the radio to hear all the terrible news from overnight, pick up the newspaper to read about it, or lie there thinking to themselves, "Oh, what am I going to do about this project or this problem today?" What is occurring during these first few minutes of your day is literally setting the stage for the kind of day you are going to have.

Take control of this. Get up an hour before your normal waking time and sit right up on the edge of the bed so you do not have the temptation of hitting the snooze alarm. Get out of bed, go brush your teeth, or whatever you need to do, and for the first fifteen minutes focus on positive events in your life and do positive visualization. There is nothing hard about it at all. See yourself achieving that goal, see yourself getting the promotion or traveling with the family. It can be one item or several items as long as a

KARMA AT WORK

———◆◆———

I hold a monthly time management seminar at a local hotel in Connecticut. A member of the wait staff is a fellow whose name is Orlando. When I first met him, he was about sixteen years old and had recently arrived in Connecticut from Puerto Rico.

One day, about an hour before our seminar was to begin, I arrived to find the room in shambles. I went into the service corridor and found Orlando. I explained the problem and how we needed to have the room set before people arrived to make the seminar run smoothly. Orlando informed me that he was not assigned to our room, but, nonetheless, he would fix the problem. He went out of his way to make it right, getting the tables set with the right number of chairs. He could have said, "Sorry, not my problem," but he didn't.

At the end of the day, I found Orlando again in the corridor and called him over. I could tell he was thinking, "What did I do wrong?"

"Remember the problem with the room this morning?" I asked.

"Yes, was everything all right?" he asked.

"It was perfect!" I told him. "You really went out of your way to get it straightened out and I know you didn't have to do it. I just wanted you to know how much I appreciate it—going out of your way like that."

What goes around comes around. You send out love in your life, and what are you going to get back? Love. You send out hate in your life, what are you going to get back? Hate.

Did Orlando appreciate those words? Sure he did. And, do you know, every month thereafter, when we are at the hotel, Orlando is always there doing that little extra to make our stay more pleasant and problem-free. Does that help me be more effective and productive? You bet it does.

◎

positive message is coming in and the negative messages are blocked out.

For the second fifteen minutes of this wakeup hour, I recommend you do some inspirational reading. Read something that you find positive and uplifting. It need not be spiritual or religious in nature, although if you are comfortable with those materials that would be fine. It may be an uplifting magazine article, a short story, or a biography.

Then, during the final thirty minutes of your wakeup hour, put on your sweats or whatever is appropriate for the weather that morning, go outside, and walk for thirty minutes and conquer your environment. While you are out there, test all of your senses. Smell things, see things, stop and just listen to your world at that time of the morning. Feel the air and taste it, too. If you notice a leaf on the ground, stop and pick it up. Examine it. Delight in its beauty. When was the last time you stopped to study a leaf? I bet you were twelve years old! See your world waking up while collecting your thoughts for the new day. What you have done in that one-hour wakeup is to take control of your mind, body, and environment—a triple reward.

Some other ways to have a more productive morning:

- *Set out your clothes the night before.* Some people struggle to get their act together in the morning be-

cause they don't know what to wear. You have to select your attire sooner or later. Why not choose
sooner? Set out your clothes tonight and give tomorrow a little jumpstart.

- *Eat breakfast.* Remember how your mom told you
  the most important meal of the day is breakfast?
  Your tank was empty. You were operating on fumes.
  So you filled the tank and off to school you went.
  These rules don't change when you turn eighteen.
  Lots of people skip breakfast because they don't
  have the time. Take the time. Fill your tank for a
  more productive day. And later on, take a lunch
  break. Many people work through their lunch period thinking they will get in more productive time.
  Get your batteries recharged, and you will increase
  your productivity.

- *Maximize your commute.* The average commute is
  about a half hour each way or an hour a day. You can
  use that time productively by listening to educa-
  tional audiotapes and CDs. You can develop your
  management skills, learn a foreign language, or improve your parenting techniques going back and

forth to work. You can listen to your favorite books on tape. One hour a day, five hours a week, and 250 hours a year. You are almost a full-time student.

Apply any of the tips you just read to your daily routine and you'll see that they are not burdensome and provide much benefit. In just a short amount of time you'll get a nose ahead of where you would have been, making small changes that produce big results, leveraging your success.

Enjoy the race.

4

ME TIME

Tuning in One Hour a Day

←——◆——→

In Chapter 3, you learned about the value of small
changes that yield big results. Now let's apply that same
concept to "me time." This is time you designate each
day for whatever it takes to achieve your goals and find balance in your life.

You have twenty-four hours a day, seven days a week, for a
total of one hundred sixty-eight hours a week. You probably
spend about a third of your time sleeping, charging up the
batteries. You spend another third of your time making your
living and paying your way. That leaves almost sixty hours a
week for you to do everything else you need to do, including eating, bathing, dressing, and other necessary tasks.

Any guess as to where about half of those sixty hours is
spent? Watching television. If you're like the average American adult, you spend almost thirty hours each week watching television. Of course, averages are made up of extremes
and you may watch more or less that the average. But there's

a good chance that you spend at least an hour or two a day in front of the TV.

Take a moment to think about your television habit. Most people would agree that the overall quality of television is not all that good. That is not to suggest that there is nothing of value on television. There is. I enjoy watching the news shows and political discussion programs. Old movies, sporting events, and clever comedy shows may be a healthy part of your week. In fact, I think it's a good idea to come home some nights and just plunk yourself down in front of the television and zone out. We all need some of that goof-off time to just unwind. But if you compare productivity to dieting and imagine that each minute is like a calorie, then television represents many empty calories.

Consider this: Watch one hour less each day to get an hour a day of "me time." Of course, there are other ways to get "me time." You could get up an hour earlier in the morning or go to bed an hour later each night. Instead of going to lunch with the same people, day after day, you could use that time as your "me time." Try to take the same hour every day. It forms an easier habit to follow.

So, what do you do with your hour of "me time"? The answer is anything. You can start an exercise program. You can spend more quality time with your family. You can create a small part-time business to augment your income. You can read more or learn a foreign language or two. You can get involved in a bowling league or a religious study class. You can even study to get a professional certification.

Take an hour each day and you'll have more than 350 hours of "me time" each year.

Here's a fact that might inspire you:

The average person, in as little as three to five years, can become recognized as a world-class expert in a topic of his or her choice just by focusing on the subject for one hour a day.

Would your future be more productive, more enjoyable, more profitable, and less stressful if you became recognized as a world-class expert in a topic of your choice? You bet! And I know this is true because I have experienced it in my own life, and I have seen it happen in the lives of others with whom I have shared this technique. One great example of a person who capitalized on his "me time" is my friend Jay.

If you compare productivity to dieting and imagine that each minute is like a calorie, then television represents many empty calories.

"ME TIME" AT WORK

Jay was an engineer with a local utility company. He had risen to a midlevel management position after twenty years of service. He wasn't doing too bad. In fact, his career was going well. The only problem was that Jay hated to go to work.

Jay wasn't exceptional in that regard. In fact, 80 percent of the workforce in the United States doesn't want to go to work. I know some jobs are worthy of that sort of contempt, but eight out of every ten Americans? And Jay was one of them. He dreaded every Monday. When he told this to me, I asked, "So why do you do it? Life is too short to drink cheap wine."

"Well," he explained, "you don't understand this industry. This is a small field. You just don't hop around from place to place. There are limited opportunities. And besides," he continued, "I have a history and a reputation in this industry. I can't just walk away from that."

"But you hate what you are doing," I reminded him.

"Yeah, but it's only nineteen years before I retire," he replied.

Nineteen years! Nineteen years until he gets his parole from this awful sentence he endures.

I inquired further, "When did you decide you wanted to become an engineer?"

He said, "When I was a freshman in high school. I was about fifteen years old."

Would you go to a fifteen-year-old today for career counseling about your future? Of course not. I mean no insult to our fifteen-year-olds, it's just that a teenager probably does not have the experiential base to counsel us in our careers. But isn't that what Jay was doing? He was holding on to the course of career path decided on by a fifteen-year-old.

Look, if you decide early on in your life to go into accounting or sales or whatever, and now, some twenty years later, you are still happy with your choice, then stick with it. But if you're no longer satisfied, change it. Fix it.

I think this has always been available to us, but never more available than it is today. We hear wonderful stories of forty- and fifty-year-old men and women going to law and medical school. We hear about professional people hanging up their shingles to go into a different business. These are exciting times.

> **The average person, in as little as three to five years, can become recognized as a world-class expert in a topic of his or her choice just by focusing on the subject for one hour a day.**

And if you're miserable at work, does that influence your home life? It sure does. In Jay's case, the effect was so bad that he and his wife were contemplating divorce. In fact, they were so close to that decision that there was no doubt they would get a divorce. The only question was who was going to file the court papers first.

Throughout this book, we discuss the tools and techniques of increasing your personal productivity. Can you increase your productivity by 20, 50, or 100 percent? Of course. Is it also possible you can decrease your productivity by 20, 50, or 100 percent? Sure. It can happen, and Jay was on the brink of experiencing a huge deficit in his productivity.

Under the law in his state, and given the circumstances of his marriage, Jay faced the likely possibility of giving up 70 percent of everything he had ever accumulated in his adult life as a property settlement. In addition, he would likely pay alimony payments in an amount equal to the 70 percent property settlement during the remainder of his soon-to-be ex-wife's life for a total of 140 percent of everything material he had earned in his adult life. His unhappiness in his career had created a serious deficit in his family life. (This is why I focus on a balanced life as the real criterium for productivity; without balance, everything falls apart.)

In the nick of time, Jay was able to pick up on my suggestion of daily "me time." He was an avid television fan, but he made a deliberate choice to leave the television off from 7:00 to 8:00 P.M. each day. He just changed one hour of his day and left the other twenty-three hours as they were.

Jay decided to devote his daily hour to improving his public speaking skills. Being an engineer by training and having a somewhat introverted personality, he found public speaking a difficult task. He knew that public speaking would help him competently and confidently express his ideas to others.

Jay bought books by Dale Carnegie and others on how to develop and improve public speaking skills. He joined Toastmasters International (www.toastmasters.org), a group that helps its members practice and improve their public speaking. He took good notes about what he learned and started to write some articles about different speaking techniques for a variety of people. Soon, he had accumulated a lot of material, enough to create a manual or two. He recorded some of this on audiotapes, videotapes, and CDs. He created a Web site. He offered items for sale to others interested in improving their public speaking skills.

Within just a couple years of embarking down this path, Jay started a business that made about ten sales a day. He and his wife came home from work each day, ate dinner as a couple, and from 7:00 to 8:00 P.M., they worked together in a bedroom converted to an office, where they downloaded the orders from the day and filled them. His monthly revenues totaled around $8,000. Expenses amounted to approximately $1,000, so he was netting around $7,000 a month.

Jay more than doubled his income since the beginning of this period without changing his job or profession. His relationship with his wife improved and he would remark to me from time to time, "I cannot believe how quickly my life turns around on a dime when I change my thinking. When my thinking was that I was a slave to my past, that I had no choices, I was stuck. When I changed my thinking to focus on the possibilities, abundance came my way."

Jay capitalized on a basic financial investment principle: If you want more wealth in your life, a better nest egg, allocate less money on the expense side of your budget and put it into the investment side. The more you invest wisely, the more likely you are to create greater wealth. Simple. We all know that. What many fail to do is apply this same principle to their own time, but it works the same way.

Recently, Jay told me he can't wait to get to work on Monday morning. In fact, he said, "I'd go there even if they didn't pay me! No, I'm not serious about that. Yes, I will take the paycheck and the benefits. It's just that I get such a kick out of going to work now that I cannot wait for Monday and a new week of work."

"Interesting," I replied, "because when I first met you, you'd almost rather have had a root canal done than go to work or spend time with your wife, for that matter. What changed? Did the world change for you?"

"No," he assured me. "The world didn't change. I changed. I still have the same job and the same wife, but what changed was me. Before all this, I went to work and was in a relationship because I had to be there. Now, I am there because I *want* to be."

Isn't that the truth? When you "have to" do anything, don't you resent it? Can't you find a number of things to keep you from having to do it? But when you want to do something, you move mountains to get it done.

Now, everything you do with your daily hour of "me time" does not have to be for a financial purpose. You can learn all about your state's history, become an expert in the topic, and give tours at the local historical society in as little as three to five years. You can become an expert on yoga or antiques or race cars from the sixties. You may not get paid for this, but imagine how such an accomplishment would make your life more fulfilling and productive.

The choice is yours. Life is a series of choices.

5

PUTTING OFF PROCRASTINATION

How to Discipline Yourself
to Do Things *Now*

———◆———

Most of us usually live somewhere between pain and pleasure. Unless we anticipate pleasure if we do something, or fear that we will be in pain if we *don't* do something, we don't do anything.

Often, many of us avoid doing the As and Bs, the items on our to-do lists that are of crucial value. Two things happen when you set aside these priorities. First, you reduce your productivity. You are just not getting the vital items done. Second, you build stress into your day because you had an expectation of how your day should go, and that expectation fell short. That stress carries over to the next day and detracts from tomorrow's productivity.

Let's say you are a student in my college business law class and this is the first day of the semester. I announce that to successfully complete this class, you have to submit on the last day of the term a forty-page, single-spaced term paper, including footnotes, bibliography, the whole works, on some dry and obscure topic like "Developments in the World's Legal Systems, 1902–1909." Pretty unpleasant assignment, huh? First, you would probably want to withdraw from this class, right? If not, do you rush home that evening to start writing? Probably not. Why? There is no pain in avoiding the assignment now because you have the entire term left and, for most, there is probably little pleasure associated with working on it. So, you procrastinate.

Suddenly, it is December 14, two days before the end of the term. You have not begun the paper. Do you start now? Probably. (What for? You still have two more days!) Is there any more pleasure with working on the paper now than there would have been on September 1? No. But if you fail to submit it in two days, you will fail the class and have to repeat it. To avoid that pain, you are now motivated to do what you have been avoiding all along.

So to do a task you need to create in your mind enough pain (which is the negative way and not my preference) or, better, enough pleasure. I believe that you are creative enough that you can always do the latter; turn your task into a game and give yourself a reward at the end for doing it. If you can master the art of making every task somehow rewarding, you will go a long way toward overcoming procrastination.

Let's put this into context.

When I was growing up, my brother and I both had the task of washing dishes after dinner. (Imagine a world without dishwashing machines.) My brother would wash one night and I would wash the next. My brother approached this unpleasant assignment from the standpoint of pain avoidance. He did it because he would be punished by our parents if he failed to do it. He would fuss and kick his way through it and therefore could pretty well count on about twenty minutes' worth of misery in his life every forty-eight hours in his foreseeable future, not because of what he had to do but because of the way he was approaching that unpleasant task.

I would approach the same task from the angle of pleasure. I was growing up during the Cold War, so as I began to wash the dishes on my night I would tell myself that these dishes had to be washed, dried, and done well in no more than twenty minutes' time or else the world would blow up in a nuclear explosion.

> **If you can master the art of making every task somehow rewarding, you will go a long way toward overcoming procrastination.**
>
> ←——•→

Was I washing dishes anymore? Not at all. I was saving the world! Did I get soap and grease all over? Sure, but what a small price to save humanity! Then, two days later when it was my turn again, I would change the rules. I would tell myself the dishes had to be done now in nineteen minutes or the world would face doom. After a few days I would tire of this game and then come up with something different.

Take that unpleasant task you have been putting off and turn it into a fun game. It will help motivate you to do whatever you have to do—now.

READ THESE TIPS NOW

Let me share with you ten more strategies to get a handle on procrastination.

1. Daily Planning

Planning your day the night before will do more to overcome procrastination than any other idea contained herein (see Chapter 2 on daily planning). Let's say it is Friday night and I think I might want to travel from Connecticut to Washington, D.C., for the weekend. I just see myself going there but I do nothing further. Saturday morning, I get up at 8:15, sleeping in a bit late because it has been a tough week. I make a pot of coffee and read the paper. The phone rings.

It is my sister from California. I have not spoken with her for some time, so we talk for the next forty-five minutes during which I tell her, "I'm going to Washington today." I get off the phone, have more coffee, and the next thing I know, it is 11:00 A.M. "Whoops! There's no way I can go to Washington now. I'm not even dressed. I have not even gotten out of my bumblebee pajamas!"

No big deal, but the point is I did not accomplish what I set out to do. Let's go back to Friday night and make a small change that will produce a big difference.

Friday night I ask myself, "What time should I arrive in Washington? Well, I'd like to be there around 3:00." Washington is about six hours from Connecticut; therefore, I will need to be on the road by 9:00 A.M. I do not want to just jump out of bed and go. I like to walk in the morning, have breakfast, and take time to pack. So, I will get up at 7:00, walk at 7:30, have breakfast at 8:00, and pack at 8:30. I do not want to drive all the way to Washington only to discover that there is a Shriners' convention in town and that there are no hotel rooms available, so I pick up the phone and make a hotel reservation. I might even make a dinner reservation and use my credit card to secure some theater tickets. Next, I get out the map and trace my route, which will include a little sightseeing detour.

Remember, your plan never owns you. You own it and it serves you. But I think you would agree, I have a much higher probability of going to Washington on Saturday morning because I took the time Friday night to do some planning. And so it is with all our days.

2. Work at a Clean Desk

Out of sight, out of mind. But remember that this works the other way around as well: When your task is in sight, it's also in mind. We can notice only the things we see around us. If you have your most important task right in front of you, that is the only thing you can focus on.

First, clean up your messy desk. Decide which day you will do it and put an action item under that day's to-do list, "Clean up the messy desk." Give it an A-1 priority so it is the primary focus of that day. Then take every piece of paper from the desk, decide when you will work on it, write it down as an action item in your day planner or your PDA's calendar on that assigned day, and file it away. By the end of the day, you may even find out what your desk is made of. (See Chapters 8 and 9 for further details on how to clean and streamline your office.)

3. Break It Down into Bites

Question: How do you eat an elephant? Answer: One bite at a time. The point here is that often we will schedule ourselves to work on a time-consuming project, say a three-hour project. The problem is that most of us do not get a solid block of three hours just to work on one thing, but we fool ourselves into thinking tomorrow will be different from yesterday or today. Then, surprise, tomorrow comes, that big chunk of time does not become available, and so we procrastinate and the cycle continues. As an alternative, why not take that first bite of the project, the first twenty or thirty minutes, and note it with "(ext)" to remind yourself to extend the next step to the next available day? It may take a bunch of days, but you will eat that whole elephant, one bite at a time. Guaranteed.

4. Chain Yourself

Let's say it is 4:00 P.M. and you have to work on a project that is long, tedious, and boring. You want to leave the office

> **If you have your most important task right in front of you, that is the only thing you can focus on.**

at 5:00, but you start to chew up the time searching for pads of paper, getting coffee, and making other "make work" until about 4:20, when you have license to say, "Well, it's too late to start on this." Sound familiar? When this occurs, *chain yourself to the desk*. I don't mean this literally. Use an imaginary chain and tell yourself that you cannot move until the task is done. Then give yourself a positive treat or reward at the end. It is a silly mind game, I know. But it also is a silly mind game to chew up the time. At least chaining yourself has a positive outcome.

5. Plan Around Interruptions

It is so much easier going with the flow than trying to buck the current. I find I get most of my interruptions early in the week. Therefore, if I plan a big A-1 item on my to-do list first thing Monday morning, I am just buying frustration because I no sooner get started than the phone rings with a client or my secretary comes in needing some information. Plan larger projects for later that week, when you anticipate fewer interruptions. Go with the flow.

6. Eat the Crust First

Many of us eat from the pointed end of a pie first, saving the crust until last because, to most, it is the less desirable part of the dessert (unless it's an all-butter crust). Some of us may not even eat the crust at all. The point here is to do the unpleasant things first. If you have something boring or tedious to do and you schedule it for late in the day, you give yourself all day to think up reasons not to do it. Schedule unpleasant items up front, first thing, and get them out of the way.

7. Avoid Filing It Under "As Soon as Possible"

Any items that are scheduled for "as soon as possible" simply wind up in the "as soon as possible" pile where they remain as long as possible. Set realistic deadlines and add on a buffer of time. Things always seem to take longer than we planned. You will give yourself a margin of error to reduce stress and, even better, you will deliver before the promised deadline and look even better. (Promise a lot but deliver a lot more.)

> **Schedule unpleasant items up front, first thing, and get them out of the way.**
>
> ←——•◆——→

8. Read the First Page Only

In college, when I would face a huge reading assignment, I would find all kinds of excuses to fritter away my time. I would make soup, rearrange my desk, and so on and never get started. Then I learned this technique: I would convince myself to read just the first page, that is all. That way I could tell the professor the next day during class that I had "read" the material. (There was some convoluted logic in all of that.) I would read that first page and the next thing I would know, it would be about 10:30 P.M. and I finished the complete assignment. There is just something about getting started that draws us into completion.

Have you ever had to clean out a basement, garage, or closet? You probably procrastinated many times before starting the task. Next time, do not tell yourself that you are going to clean the entire closet. Just tell yourself you are going to do only the shoes or just the blouses. Start the task and it is likely that you will be drawn into it and complete it.

9. Be Early

When you are late, you procrastinate. You miss things, meetings have to be rescheduled, and you are rushed and unfocused. A "late" person is someone who does not have a good relationship with the clock. He or she is ten minutes late today, twenty minutes late tomorrow.

The solution? Set your watch ahead twenty minutes. Be conscious of the time. Leave early. There is a "lateness acceptability factor" in our culture that says if you are late some of the time because of traffic, the weather, or personal circumstances, then it is okay. But if you are late some of the time, what that makes you look like is average, just like everyone else. What if you are one of those people who is on time, all the time? Will that make you look different? Sure. Not a big difference, but remember, you only have to be a nose ahead of the competition to get more results.

10. Avoid the Curse of Perfectionism

We instinctively allocate a limited amount of time to accomplish a particular result so there is time for other things. It spins off the twenty-eighty rule, which suggests that we put in 20 percent of the available time to achieve an 80 percent result.

> **Start the task and it is likely that you will be drawn into it and complete it.**

For example, this Saturday I would like to clean my basement. I have ten hours, from 8:00 A.M. to 6:00 P.M., available. I cannot spend all ten hours on this one project because I will get nothing else done. So, I plan on spending a couple of hours (20 percent) to accomplish the result of a clean basement (clean enough, anyway). It will not be perfect, but it will be satisfactory and I will have time to spend with the kids, do yard work, or take a nap. If 20 percent of the time (two hours) accomplished 80 percent of the result, to squeeze out the additional 20 percent result, I would have to put in 80 percent (eight hours) of time. It takes time to throughly clean every corner and crevice that no one will ever see! I'd rather have a basement that is 80 percent clean and move on to something else.

Those who suffer from the curse of perfectionism claim an 80 percent result is never satisfactory. It has to be perfect. It has to be 100 percent. If we are talking about a quantifiable task such as adding a column of figures, perfection applies. Either the column adds up to the correct amount or it does not. However, when dealing with qualitative items such as cleaning a basement or polishing up a proposal, there really cannot be perfection.

Perfectionism can be a treatable disorder. I read recently about a housewife who lived with her husband in their small three-bedroom home. In the morning, she went to the refrigerator to get a glass of juice and noticed some dust accumulating under the refridgerator. She got her little broom out to clean it up. Then she got the vacuum out with the skinny extension. But that wasn't enough so she got her husband out of bed and the two dragged the refrigerator out of its slot to do a really good job of cleaning those dust bunnies. But then she noticed the tile was coming up where the refrigerator was, so she began to mix the cement to fix that problem. Then she noticed the molding around the refrigerator slot was chipped, so she got out the paint and brushes to fix that. This went on until 11:00 P.M.

This was her typical day. She spent about eighteen hours a day, seven days a week doing these household chores, setting aside every other important task in her life. And then she went to a therapist, and the reason she sought treatment was that she was still anxious that her work was not good enough.

That's an extreme case, but I think most of us suffer from a mild case of perfectionism from time to time. As you approach each task in life, allocate a reasonable amount of time to achieve a reasonable level of success and then move on to other tasks. There are plenty of other things to do with your time.

Don't let your life be controlled by spur-of-the-monent impulses for pleasure or pain avoidance. There will always be something that you want to put off for later, but if you manage that impulse you'll find that you'll stop missing deadlines and suffering from last-minute emergencies that diminish the quality of your work, your life, and your over-all productivity.

6

ANTICIPATE THE UNANTICIPATED
MANAGING INTERRUPTIONS

←——•◆•——→

Wilfredo Pareto, an Italian economist, discovered that about 20 percent of the companies in an economy are responsible for generating 80 percent of the gross national product and the remaining 80 percent of the companies generate the other 20 percent of the gross national product. This idea became known as the Pareto Principle, or the twenty-eighty rule.

No, don't worry, this chapter is not about macroeconomics. But the twenty-eighty rule has a lot of relevance to our daily lives. If you belong to any organization (the PTA, a religious organization, a youth group, etc.), you have probably noticed how 20 percent of the members are there 80 percent of the time, doing 80 percent of the work, and the remaining 80 percent of the members are there 20 percent of the time, doing 20 percent of the work. Within your family, have you ever noticed how 20 percent of your relatives give you 80 percent of your headaches? How 20 percent of a typical sales force will produce 80 percent of the sales and 80 percent of the sales force will produce 20 percent of the sales? Real life may not always work with exact mathematical precision, but, typically, it is the small group of whatever that produces the big chunk of results.

This same rule holds true for interruptions. Most people find that about 20 percent of the people they interact with will be responsible for about 80 percent of the interruptions and the other 80 percent of the people will deliver the other 20 percent of the interruptions. These interruptions can throw you off track throughout your day.

An interruption is an unanticipated event. You do not know when it is coming. That is what makes it an interruption. They come to us in one of two ways, either in person or electronically: telephones, pagers, and e-mail. Interruptions are both good and bad. There are A- and B-level interruptions, which, by definition, are crucial and important. They are not the problem.

The problem are the C- and D-level interruptions, which, by definition, have little or no value. To the extent you spend time on these items, they keep you from accomplishing the more important items, thereby decreasing your productivity.

YOUR INTERRUPTIONS LOG

To get a handle on the interruptions problem, we need to define it and determine when and how it happens. To do so, I recommend you run an interruptions log for a period of three to five days. If you run the log for a day or so, you may get a distorted sense of what is happening. If you do it for the recommended three to five days, you'll get a more accurate picture.

There's nothing fancy about it at all. Take a pad of paper and across the top write "Interruptions Log" and then make six columns:

- *Date*—the date the interruption occurs.

- *Time*—when the interruption begins.

- *Who*—the person who interrupted you.

- *What*—a note or two to remind you of what the interruption was about.

- *Length*—the actual time it took.

- *Rating*—the value of the interruption, using the A, B, C, and D prioritizing system. Put down the value to you, not the value to the interrupter. (To the interrupter, the value is almost always an A.) Be brutally candid. No one needs to see your log, so you do not have to account for your rating with anyone.

I know it is a pain in the neck, and elsewhere, to be bothered with logging interruptions, but it *takes only a few seconds to log in each interruption immediately after it occurs*. If you wait until the end of the day to fill it out, you will not remember.

Without further interruption, let us go back to our log. It is Monday, October 16, 9:02 A.M., and Fran stops by my desk. She has a new way to get that Anderson research done in half the time. What a great interruption! This is going to save me time in the future. I would probably rate this as an A. In fact, I would like to encourage more interruptions like this. We discuss this for the next twelve minutes. The log entry would look like this:

Date	Time	Who	What	Length	Rating
10/16	9:02	Fran	Anderson res.	12	A

Then, at 9:45, Bill comes by to complain about how the baseball season is progressing and how the Yankees could have done better this season. We spend fifteen minutes in this discussion. My next entry would look like this:

Date	Time	Who	What	Length	Rating
10/16	9:02	Fran	Anderson res.	12	A
10/16	9:45	Bill	Whining	15	D

I rate Bill's interruption as a D. Is Bill a D? No! He is a great guy, worthy of my love and respect. It is just that the time spent with him is a D. There is a difference.

From your viewpoint, maybe spending that fifteen minutes with Bill had some value or a lot of value. Perhaps you are interested in baseball or maybe you are the new kid on the block and Bill is your boss and a little schmoozing and rapport building has value to you. You put down what you think it was worth to you. It's your time.

Having run the interruptions log for three to five days, you have accumulated a lot of useful information. First, you will determine how many interruptions you are getting. Some discover that they do not get interrupted nearly as often as they thought, which is a good thing. Most, however, discover that they get interrupted far more than they ever imagined.

> **In an eight-hour day, the average person experiences forty-eight interruptions.**

LOOK FOR PATTERNS

Look for patterns when interruptions occur. In an eight-hour day, the average person experiences forty-eight interruptions. Examine the contents of your log.

1. When?

Are they early or late in the day? Early or late in the week? Spotting patterns can help you to plan larger tasks around and away from interruptions to avoid procrastinating the important items.

2. Who?

Here, most will find evidence of the Pareto Principle, the twenty-eighty rule, at work. Most people find that about 20 percent of the people they interact with will be responsible for about 80 percent of the interruptions and the other 80 percent of the people will deliver the other 20 percent of the interruptions.

3. What?

This column reminds us of the issues discussed—just a note, a word or two. Are you being interrupted for the same thing all the time?

4. Length?

Along with "The check's in the mail" and "Trust me," there's "This will just take a minute." *It never takes "just a minute," does it?* The average interruption takes approximately five minutes and interruptions occur, on average, once every eight minutes (your actual mileage may vary). One interruption every eight minutes calculates out to around six interruptions an hour. When divided by sixty minutes per hour, that is four hours out of an eight-hour day, or 50 percent of the workday.

5. Rating?

The last column is most revealing. Most people who have conducted their Interruptions Log and reported back to us discover that only about 20 percent of their interruptions were of the A and B variety and that 80 percent were of the C and D variety. (This may be high or low for you. Run your own log to test your actual experience.) If you spend four hours on interruptions and 80 percent are Cs and Ds, that is a bit more than three hours a day going down the drain on things that have little or no value.

THE SOLUTION

What is the solution? Easy. Go to your Bills, the people who repeatedly interrupt and waste your time, and ask for their cooperation. I'm not going to put words in your mouth. Use the words that are comfortable for you, but perhaps the following could be useful: "Bill, I didn't realize how much of your time I was wasting each day! How about if we get together after work? Maybe we can get a beer and I'll pay." Or "Bill, I have to run to a meeting in five minutes. Can I catch you later?" You use the words that are comfortable for you. This is the easy part.

You might be thinking I am getting awfully picky about Bill. Am I such a time management nut that I can't spend fifteen minutes out of my precious day to talk about baseball? Sure, if Bill is an occasional and infrequent interrupter, I am not going to be concerned. It is not a perfect world. We will waste time every day; it's a fact of life. But let's say that every day, around the same time, Bill comes by to complain about baseball, the price of hay in Denmark, or whatever. Add it up: fifteen minutes a day is seventy-five minutes a week. An hour and a quarter. Over the next year, that adds up to more than sixty-two hours. If I told you that you would have to sit at a table for the next sixty-two hours and listen to Bill moan and groan about whatever was on his mind, you would think I was crazy.

Will you be able to correct all the C and D interrupters? No, of course not. There may be situations where you feel uncomfortable confronting someone like Bill. Perhaps some interruptions just don't bother you. Maybe baseball is your most important priority. It's okay. You are not a machine.

Do not worry about recapturing all the lost interruption time. If you recapture just half of it, that is 1.5 hours each day or 7.5 hours each week; over the next year, that is 375 hours or 9 work weeks coming your way and it is all for free, with a little effort on your part.

TELEPHONE INTERRUPTIONS

We are slaves to the telephone. The phone rings, we stop what we are doing, and we answer it, responding like Pavlov's dog at the sound of the bell. It would be wonderful if every time we picked it up the call was important, but we know it is not.

When all of my children were living at home, having a weeknight family dinner was a once-a-week event, given the cheerleading practice, basketball games, meetings, and other activities we all had. We'd pull it off about once a week, and this family time was important to us. Nancy, my wife, would prepare a family dinner and then everyone would sit down at the table to eat it. And what always happened in the middle of it? The phone rang. Everything would stop. My daughter would rush to the phone because it might be her boyfriend, my oldest son would tease her because it might be the boyfriend, and, meanwhile, my youngest would munch away at his meal.

Then I would hear the three most dreaded words at this time of the day, "Dad, for you." And when I got on the phone, who would it be? Typically, some insurance person or fund-raising telemarketer offering me the opportunity to part with some of my money. Now, I do not begrudge those who use the telephone to make their living. But those calls are Ds. The time with family around the dinner table is an A. Here I am giving up A time so I can go spend some D time. It happens all the time.

Now we have a new rule at home. When we sit down for a family dinner and the phone rings (and you know it will), *we do not answer it.* To some this sounds like heresy. Then an interesting thing happens. When you let the phone ring, it just rings. And it continues to ring until it does not ring anymore (or voice mail picks it up). And that is about all there is to it. If it's important, the caller will call back or leave a message. They always do, and you and I know that most of the time it is not important.

One other thing I discovered is that the number of calls we receive between 6:00 and 6:30 P.M. has decreased as word has gotten out to the 20 percent who are making 80 percent of the calls. ("Oh, don't call their house. Their father is a time management nut and he won't let them answer the phone.") You teach people how to treat you by the way you allow them to treat you. If you make yourself available for every call at any time of day or night, you teach people to call at all times.

The same phone policy applies at work. I use the phone extensively in my seminar business. I typically get twenty-five inbound phone calls a day. Whenever someone calls and hears that I am in the office, he or she wants to speak to me directly and immediately. Unfortunately, if I take every call, I will get nothing else done.

I have a few solutions:

- *If possible, have someone else field your calls.* My secretary is splendid and knowledgeable and can field many of the questions. If I am on another line or

> **If you make yourself available for every call at any time of day or night, you teach people to call at all times.**

with someone, we take a message. We also make it a point to return all phone calls the same day. (We do not succeed 100 percent of the time, but we are pretty good.)

- *Use voice mail.* But, frankly, some people occasionally get offended if they always get your voice mail. No one wants to be put off, because his or her concerns are immediate.

- *Use caller ID.* Screen your calls by only picking up the phone for relevant calls.

When I am traveling away from the office, I call my office to get the messages from the previous twenty-four hours. When callers are told, "He's not here, but he will get back to you once he calls in for his messages," only five people out of twenty-five will consider their call important enough to leave a message. That is 20 percent. Yet, if I were in the office when the call came in and the caller knew it, he or she might be offended by a delay in speaking with me. That tells you a lot about how urgent and important those inbound phone calls really are.

Voice mail, home answering machines, caller ID answering services, and screening calls are all good alternatives to dropping everything when the phone rings, particularly if the call will throw you off track and keep you from more important tasks. But simply ignoring the phone works best. You can always return a call at a time that works for *you*.

—————◆————→

The bottom line is that you need to anticipate the unanticipated, and interruptions are those events that you can predict will throw you off track if you let them. Exercise control over the interruptions that threaten your productivity by thoughtfully dealing with them before they happen and developing skills to contain and control them when they do.

7

DELEGATE THE SHIRT
OFF YOUR BACK

WORKING WITH OTHERS TO
ACCOMPLISH YOUR GOALS

———— ✦ ————

That shirt you are wearing, could you have created it from scratch? I mean, plant the cotton seed, harvest the cotton, spin it, dye it, cut it, and sew it to produce the result called a shirt? Sure. Would you have wanted to do that? Perhaps not, but could you? Yes. How many hours of your time would have been involved to duplicate that shirt from scratch? Perhaps hundreds or thousands. Luckily, you have another option: You can go to a store, plunk down $30, and walk out with the shirt ready made for you.

Is this an example of delegation? Sure it is. Here's another one: Do you have mail delivered to your home? Could you go to the post office, rent a box, and drive your car there every day to pick up your mail? Sure. But you probably made the decision that this was not the best use of your time, so you delegated it. Did you buy a sandwich and drink for lunch today? Could you have grown the lettuce, ground the flour, baked the bread, and cultured the cheese? Sure. But you delegated it instead.

Imagine life without delegation and this was exactly the way the world worked up until about 300 years ago. If you wanted something in your life, you (and your small community) had to produce it. You wanted clothing? You had to make it. You wanted food? You had to grow it or kill it. You wanted housing? You could not go to the local real estate agent, look at some pictures, sign some papers, and move in. You had to clear the land and build the house yourself. You wanted transportation? You could not stroll into your Saturn dealership. You had to cut down some trees, build a wagon, and train a horse.

If you look at the development of personal wealth throughout history, up until relatively recently, people were not a whole lot better off financially than at any other time since the dawn of civilization. Then what happened? The Industrial Revolution. The idea of mechanized manufactur-

> **If you want to achieve great results in your life, you have to delegate more and more because there is only a limited amount of time in a week.**
>
> ←—•→

ing processes that permitted companies to produce products on a mass scale at relatively cheap prices required companies to pay relatively good wages so people could buy the items to produce profits, enabling companies to put out even more products, cycling upward to where we are today in terms of personal wealth.

If you had to produce everything you already have in your life today from scratch, you would not have 95 percent of what you have now. You would have only about 5 percent of the results you currently enjoy. So the answer to whether or not you delegate is yes, perhaps in ways you had not thought of before. The question now is: How far do you want to go with it? With some 6 billion people in the world, the possibilities are endless. If you want to achieve great results in your life, you have to delegate more and more because there is only a limited amount of time in a day.

DO THE MATH

Delegation is plugging into someone else's time stream when you do not have the time or the expertise to produce a result. Look at it this way:

You have 168 hours in your week. No more, no less. Subtract 56 hours for sleep and that leaves 112 available hours each week to achieve your results. Then take out a factor for work, preparation time, and commuting in the pursuit of your financial goals, an average of fifty-five hours a week, and you are down to *fifty-seven hours a week* to do all the other things you need to do, including eating!

If you had twice as much time in your week (say 224 available hours versus 112), you could get twice as much done, at least in theory. But it is not a workable theory because, no matter how you slice it, you have only 112 hours left after sleep (unless you choose to sleep less, which I don't recommend).

But what if you plug into someone else's time stream? How about if you get someone else to produce results for you? You accomplish the same results.

Most people I speak to do not feel they are good delegators or do not feel they have the opportunity to delegate much. The hardest part about delegation is simply letting go. We take great pride in doing the job ourselves. My wife, Nancy, and I have had this discussion many times over the years. When our four children were all at home, laundry was a big task for the six of us and Nancy would do it all, spending two to three hours a day on it. It was not as though she

> **The hardest part about delegation is simply letting go.**
>
> ←——◆◆——→

did not get some satisfaction from it, but oftentimes she would complain that she did not have enough time to do other things, like spend time with her hobbies. My response was to delegate by letting the kids do it. Her response was, "By the time I show them how to do it, I could just as well have done it myself." But that is a trap. If you give a person a fish, he or she feeds him- or herself for a day. If you teach a person to fish, he or she feeds him- or herself for a lifetime. The same goes for washing clothes.

You need not be a math major to figure out that it makes no sense to spend an hour showing someone how to complete a ten-minute task. The expense is not justified. But when you apply the concept of investment and understand that one hour invested will save you ten minutes, ten minutes every day, then your investment is repaid in a week and you now get an ongoing dividend of ten more free minutes in a day.

Invest time over the next month delegating just six ten-minute tasks and you recapture one hour a day.

Nancy would say, "But they'll just mess it up, putting the red jeans in with the white underwear and the underwear will come out pink." My response was, "So what?" That is the process we all have to go through to learn. Imagine a new rule in life that says no three-year-old can make a peanut butter sandwich until he or she knows how to make a peanut butter sandwich! Remember the first time you, or your child, made a peanut butter sandwich? It was not exactly a gourmet, five-star delight. But some of our three-year-olds today will grow up to be five-star chefs at major restaurants. They will have to mess up a lot of peanut butter sandwiches along the way to get there.

Delegation is not "dumping," it's just unloading a problem onto someone else. Delegation is giving it to the right person. It may also involve giving him or her the tools to do it, providing him or her the support he or she needs, allowing him or her to make decisions and errors, and having a feedback process to maximize the results.

HOW TO DELEGATE

The following are some ways in which to take advantage of delegation.

1. Get a Staff

At work, if you have staff members—assistants, interns, para-professionals, or others—use them. People tend to rise or sink to your level of expectation. If you are always telling

> **Invest time over the next month delegating just six routine ten-minute tasks and you recapture one hour a day.**

those staff members around you, "Better let me handle this," "This is too important," or "I'm the only one to do this," you are sending out a message that they are incompetent.

I remember when our oldest daughter, Jennifer, was fifteen months old. One Sunday morning she had gotten into her dresser drawer, dug out a sweater, and tried to put it on. She had a leg down one sleeve and the other sleeve was tucked in at the waist. She came into our bedroom and woke us up because she had something important to tell us. "I dressed myself." Sure, she made a mess of it, but even at that young age we all have a need to achieve. Nurture it. Take advantage of it. Delegate all you can to the lowest levels of your staff and the staff will rise to the occasion.

You might be thinking this is a great idea for those who have a staff, but what if you say, "I am the staff! I have no one to delegate to." If you have no staff to delegate to and you know that if you did they could help solve some of your time management issues, then why not think of ways to get staff? Who can be your staff, if only for a half hour once a week or in a time of need?

The idea of a staff doesn't apply only to support staff. Depending upon your situation, your spouse, significant other, children, family, friends, and co-workers are likely to help, if you ask. People, especially those who care for you the most, want to and will help, if you ask, which leads us to the next tip.

2. Ask for Help

Asking is one of the most powerful things we can do. The Bible talks about it. "Ask and ye shall receive." It does not say, "Sit there and think about it and maybe it will come your way." Now, it is all in how you ask. I have found that if you offer people something that is worth more than what you want in return, the world will beat a path to your door. Offer to do something first for a person that is worth more to him or her than what you need from him or her. For example, "How about if I process your invoices and in return you complete this call list?" It works. When you do have spare time, always offer to help someone else. Your generosity will pay off when you are in a time of need. If you ask and they say no, then you wind up not getting the assistance you did not have in the first place. I know the real world. At home, your wife or husband might say no because he or she is too busy as well. At work, budget cuts and hiring freezes exist, so if at the office you ask for a staff person and the management says no, then you can try the next technique, reverse delegation.

3. Practice Reverse Delegation

An engineer once attended my time management seminar. He was buried in work and, like most of us when we get into a crisis, he had to pay for it out of his hide by putting in more time. He was taking work home, working on the weekends, and getting out of balance with his family. He followed my suggestion of putting all his responsibilities down on paper and discovered he had about twelve weeks of work to do in about six weeks.

He was overcommitted by two to one. This situation is common because we are all taught to say yes when our boss asks us to do something (you don't get too far in this world by saying no all the time). He felt his solution was to get a staff engineer to whom he could delegate certain items. His boss explained that with the budget and hiring freezes, this was not possible.

So, he reverse delegated. "Okay. Which one of these assignments do you want back? And which deadlines can I extend so that deadlines match commitments?"

These are fair questions. You have a right to ask them. Oftentimes, people misplace their loyalty to an organization or to their clients and customers by saying, "I'll do whatever it takes to do this job." That is commendable. I believe in the work ethic. I believe we have to do more than what we are being paid for now if we ever expect to get a raise. All I am saying is that if you are on a path that is eventually going to burn you out and then you leave, is that a good thing for your organization?

So much of the turnover in our workforce is attributable

to burnout. And every time we change a job, does that interfere with our personal productivity? Sure it does. We lose seniority and contacts, have a new learning curve to overcome, and get set backward.

My engineer friend got his boss to agree to take back a couple of items and adjust the deadlines for the rest. He got out of his time management crisis.

Now, how do you reverse delegate if you *are* the boss? Whenever this happened in our office, I would often get caught up in others' problems and have to push aside my own priorities. For example, Kathy, my office manager, came to me one afternoon with a stressed-out expression on her face. "The Subway Corp. wants us to conduct a time management seminar during the first week of November and that's the same week the People's Bank wants us and I don't know what to do about it."

With some experience, I now know that before I jump in and take over this newly presented challenge, I must ask the reverse delegation question, "So what do you think we ought to do about it?" *You* is a powerful word in that ques-

> **When you do have spare time, always offer to help someone else. Your generosity will pay off when you're in need.**

tion. *You* instills confidence, raises people up, and creates independency. Many times when delegating, we use the weak word *I*, which creates dependency.

Kathy responded, "Well, we could move the People's Bank seminar over to that available slot we have in January or maybe I could combine the Subway Corp.'s seminar with the Philips Medical seminar." And I replied, "Those are both great ideas. You just let me know which one you choose." Kathy left my office with a smile on her face, feeling empowered.

My experience has been that I reverse delegate more than 50 percent of the problems presented to me, keeping my time free to focus on my to-do list.

4. Get a Gopher

I have gotten a lot of mileage out of hiring gophers over the years. Each of us has ten to fifteen hours a week of minutia, low-level tasks that need to be done. You have to go to the grocery store, clean the house, mow the lawn, and put gas in the car. It all has to be done and to the extent that you enjoy doing it, that is fine. Perhaps grocery shopping on Saturday morning permits you to meet and greet the neighbors and have quality time with a family member. All I am suggesting is this: If you are spending ten to fifteen hours a week doing these rather low-level items and then complain that you do not have enough time to do the things you really want to do, than maybe you have a choice.

The choice is to hire a college assistant (or local teenager or personal assistant). The job title is "gopher" because the person is going to "go for" this and "go for" that. (It is an affectionate term.) I recommend a college student versus a high school student because you will have greater flexibility in scheduling and will probably hire a more mature person, although I have hired high school students in this role with great success. To recruit someone, simply call the placement offices at the local schools and colleges, get their fax number or e-mail address, and send out a simple notice for their jobs book. Students love this type of job. It gives them more freedom than the fast-food type of employment. You will receive a flood of applications.

You are looking for three qualities:

- *A level-headed, responsible person because the job is not closely supervised*
- *Access to a car and a good driving record*
- *All-purpose skills*

Delegate the grocery shopping, laundry, mowing the grass, and cleaning the house to this person. This will free up your time to do things that are more meaningful to your lifetime success. Guaranteed.

Beyond these three things, if the individual has ever held a paintbrush in his or her hands, it is a bonus. You are not going to get a master craftsman at this level.

The pay scale should be competitive with other entry-level jobs in retail and fast food. (Do not forget to check with your accountant about paying any appropriate taxes.)

———— ✦ ————

The starting point of delegation is each night during your daily planning session. Examine all of your appointments and scheduled events and all of your discretionary items listed on your to-do lists on the days you have scheduled to do them. Ask yourself this question: Is this the best use of my time to personally attend this appointment or to do this discretionary item? If it is, go ahead and do it. If it is not, try to think of a way to delegate it and free up your time to do something more meaningful.

There is a big difference in time commitment between "I do it" and "It gets done." Which is more important? "It gets done." Sure, it is great to do things yourself, but remember, you have only a small amount of time to spare. Be careful how you spend it.

8

STREAMLINING

Tips for Systematizing
Your Everyday Life

I cannot tell you how many times I sat at my keyboard and typed out directions to our time management seminar in Connecticut. I received an urgent e-mail the day before the seminar from one of the attendees. "Don, I lost the directions to your seminar tomorrow. How do I get there?" I'd grab that fire hose and reply, "You take route 8 south and get off at exit 12. At the end of the ramp, take a right . . ." and send the response off. Phew! Problem solved. The customer was served.

Well, until the next month when the same request came my way and I had to retype the same directions all over again. Why? Because I forgot to save the directions in a Word document that I could later cut and paste in an e-mail to subsequent requestors in a fraction of the time it takes to type them all over again. When I'm responding to a request, I am down there in the trenches thinking only about how to serve this client and solve this problem in this moment. My thinking also should include ways to preserve and leverage this task for greater productivity in the future.

Most of us waste time because we don't have systems in place for our most repetitive tasks. The solution is to systematize. Systematizing is the simple procedure of creating a routine way of responding to the myriad tasks that you encounter regularly. It means taking a look at all you do and always asking yourself how it all can be done more efficiently.

WAYS TO SYSTEMATIZE

The following are a few places you may begin to streamline your life.

1. Create Templates for Everyday Communications

Do you find yourself sending the same e-mail or cover letter over and over again? If so, save these texts as templates. I have dozens of such documents in my computer. These include many of the articles that people request through our Web site, form letters I send out for business and personal contacts, and standard informational documents such as directions to our office and seminars. Most of the information I need to send to respond to my e-mails is there or easily modified and tailored so that I don't have to type out repetitive information. You might also prepare thank-you letters, requests for more information, letters to politicians, and other standard communications as templates for further use.

2. Use a Single Calendar System

Some people use as many as a dozen ways of tracking their appointments and scheduled events and their to-do list items. They have one calendar for work and one for personal things. They have Post-it notes sticking on their computers reminding them what must be done. The dentist appointment card is on the bathroom mirror and the dry cleaner claim slip is hanging from the visor in the car. The softball schedule is on the refrigerator and they have several other commitments in their heads. Boil this all down to a single system. (See Chapter 2 for details on month-at-a-glance calendars.) I use Day-Timer products, but whatever product you feel comfortable with is fine. PDAs are really neat, and as they evolve, we will all no doubt use electronic devices to control our calendars and to communicate. No matter what format

> **Most of us waste time because we don't have systems in place for our most repetitive tasks.**
>
> ⟵——◆◆——⟶

or device you use, make it a simple, singular master system into which you record all appointments and scheduled events and your to-do list items, both business and personal.

3. Create a Simple Filing System

A filing system's purpose is easy retrieval of key information. Over the years, I have experimented with a variety of filing systems. We have used color-coded files, filing by subject matter, and sophisticated retrieval devices. It really got complex and was more trouble than it was worth. Now, I maintain two sets of files, "active" and "dead," all filed alphabetically. I have about two hundred active files, client accounts, and projects to work on. They are filed alphabetically in drawers that are within easy reach of my desk. It sounds like a lot, but I am reasonably familiar with the contents and what is where. When the file is concluded, it's filed alphabetically in the dead files. Simple. No more color-coding stickers. No more complex solutions to a simple problem.

4. Clean Up Your Desk or Work Area

Studies show that the person who works at a messy desk spends, on average, one to one and a half hours a day looking for things or being distracted by things. That's seven and a half hours a week! And it's not a solid block of an hour and a half, but a minute here and a minute there, and, like a leaky hot water faucet, drip, drip, drip, it doesn't seem like a major loss, but at the end of the day, you're losing gallons of hot water that you're paying to heat. (See Chapter 9 for more details on how to organize your office.)

If you have ever visited the office of a top manager, you'll notice that person is typically working in a clean environment. Many would attribute this result to that person's access to other staff members to delegate much of his or her workload. While there may be some truth to this, in most cases, if we went back some years in that person's career, he or she was probably working with a clean desk back then, which gave him or her the focus he or she needed to be promoted to where he or she is today.

5. Make Your Physical Surroundings Workable

I work within three circles around my desk and workspace.

Circle one is within arm's reach and contains all that I

> **Studies show that the person who works at a messy desk spends, on average, one to one and a half hours a day searching for things and being distracted by things.**

need on a daily basis to do what I have to do. This includes my computer, current file, telephone, pencil sharpener, package of Life Savers, pens and pencils, and the like.

Circle two is a step or two away from my desk. In it are the less frequently used items such as the photocopier, shredder, and files.

Circle three is out of sight. There I place the files and materials I use infrequently or not at all, put away out of sight and out of mind yet available if I need them.

Look at your setup. Consider moving the fax machine closer (or farther away) from your desk. Put the most frequently used and needed files within arm's reach and the less frequently required items farther out. Have adequate space at your desk to do what you need to do. You might even remove some unnecessary items that might distract you.

6. Set Up a Functional Briefcase

I travel a lot and am often out of my office at seminars or meetings. I always tote along my briefcase. Besides the stuff I need for where I am going, I stock my briefcase with many neat things like a calculator, a pocket map of the United States, basic office supplies (writing pads, pens, yellow markers, small stapler, paper clips, stamps, and a few envelopes), blank checks, a few deposit slips, a paperback book I have been intending to read, and at least one A-1 project I can work on if I get stuck in traffic or at the airport or am waiting for the meeting to begin.

In fact, I secretly welcome unexpected delays from time to time to get done what is difficult to get done at the office, like writing and serious goal planning. When the world wants to force you to spend D time, you can convert that to A time, if you are prepared.

7. Schedule Maintenance

I met a salesman in one of my seminars. He had been working for months to close a sale that would earn him $5,000 in commissions. On the day of the closing, the low-level pain in his tooth exploded into a throbbing problem that required him to cancel the closing and lose the sale and the commission to go to the dentist for a cure to a problem that he could have resolved weeks beforehand.

The equipment you use, your computer, your car, and, oh yeah, even *you* need maintenance. Preventive maintenance is a lot less costly than necessitated maintenance. You know your car must be serviced. Why wait for a breakdown to get it done and spend more time on what could have been accomplished in less time? (You still need a tune-up, but now you have to wait for the tow truck to arrive.)

Regular medical and dental checkups save huge amounts of time in our future by fixing small conditions before they become major costly issues. (This is what I mean by balancing your life. If you neglect one area, such as your health, it will diminish your productivity in all other areas.)

Schedule all these routine weekly, monthly, or yearly activities into your calendar and to-do lists.

8. Maximize Technology

There is so much technology available today that can streamline systems and leverage your productivity. However, it can also work against you if you adopt technology just for technology's sake. The key is to use these devices when they work for you, and turn them off when you need to focus on something else.

———————————— *Cell Phones* ————————————

I have a cell phone but I do not give out the number. My wife and kids know it. I would have to look it up. I do not want to pick up incoming calls through my cell phone and have to carry a live phone with me all the time. I would rather use my office voice mail system (see Chapter 6 on managing interruptions). So, I turn on my cell phone only when I need it.

You can save time text messaging on your cell phone because text messages tend to be brief and to the point. Be careful that they do not drift into mere idle chatter: "How are you?" "I am fine." "Where are you?" "I am on the bus." "What are you doing?" "I am text messaging you."

PDAs

Palms, BlackBerries, and other personal digital assistants are terrific productivity tools when used appropriately to respond to e-mails in real time, make phone calls, and manage your contact lists and daily schedule—all in one place. In fact, they work so well that you might fall into the trap of checking your e-mail *all* the time. Discipline yourself. Turn the gadget off after hours.

Computers

It goes without saying that computers can streamline your everyday life. Use them for creating and filing your work, conducting electronic banking, writing e-mails, doing Internet research, and much more. E-mail may be a better alternative to a phone call to a long-winded person. The search capabilities on computers allow you to find files with

> You can save time text messaging on your cell phone because text messages tend to be brief and to the point.

a key word or by date or subject, which can save you time. Beware the charms of the Internet, however. More and more people are wasting hours online reading blogs and gossip sites in the same way they waste time watching TV. Set a limit to the time you spend surfing the Web and stick to it.

(Read more details about saving time on e-mail, the phone, and other technologies in Chapter 9.)

9. Always Have Adequate Supplies on Hand

Some people fritter away their productive time looking for supplies such as a pen or a pad of paper or staples for their stapler. At home, there's nothing worse than starting a recipe only to realize that you used up all the eggs in the morning omelet.

I used to be one of those people. Some time ago, I was about to leave my office at 11:00 A.M. to catch the train to New York City for an important afternoon meeting. Suddenly, my phone rang. It was a call from a potential client who needed me to fax some information to him immediately. I cranked it out and pressed "print." Oops. The ink cartridge was dry. A trip to the supply closet revealed that I had grabbed the last ink cartridge for my printer a few weeks ago. While I drove across town to the office supply store, I called, via my cell phone, to reschedule my appointment in New York City. Fortunately, I was able to reschedule my meeting to another date and time. But look at the stress that could have been avoided had I kept a spare printer cartridge on hand!

Take a monthly inventory of all your routine shopping items to avoid multiple inconvenient trips to the store. For office supplies, I keep a three-by-five inventory card in my day planner for Staples, the office supply store. When I get low on a particular supply item, I add it to the list. Then, every couple of weeks, I make one trip to Staples rather than making many frequent trips.

———◆———

Make it an ongoing practice to look at everything you do and analyze how it is done and how it can be done better. You will find yourself making small improvements, saving a few minutes here and there, that when strung together will help you to recoup time for more productive use. Once streamlined, you'll go faster.

> **Take a monthly inventory of all your routine shopping items to avoid multiple inconvenient trips to the store.**
>
> ———◆———

Information is the currency of
success in the Information Age
—but there's an infinite amount
of information and only so much
time. In this section, you will learn
how to manage and absorb more of
the right kind of information, faster
and more efficiently.

PART 2 INFORMATION

9

SHRINK YOUR INBOX

TIPS FOR REDUCING AND
MANAGING INFORMATION

In every day of your working life there's a good chance that you'll be bombarded with telephone calls, voice mails, e-mails, regular mail, junk mail, memos, pamphlets, faxes, books, and even a FedEx package or two. It's all information. Some of it is helpful and necessary to your goals. Much of it is wasteful and distracting. On average, the typical businessperson receives about 150 communications each day, and only a fraction of that information is relevant.

If you're like most people, you pay attention to the most urgent stuff and the rest sits in a pile on your desk or e-mail or voice mail inbox. Occasionally, you might rummage through your pile and do a few of the things that you did not do yesterday. Regardless, the pile grows. On the third day, you repeat the process, dealing with some of the new stuff, some of the stuff from days before, and maybe a thing or two that is slipping through the cracks. The mere thought of all those papers and unanswered calls and e-mails creates stress, reminding you of all the things that are not getting done.

Sound familiar? Here's how to deal with it better.

HOW TO SHRINK YOUR INBOX

1. Avoid Receiving Information You Don't Need

The best way to deal with paper overload is simply never to have it. A lot of annoying paperwork can be eliminated by getting off memo distribution lists, mailing lists, and the like. First, look at what comes your way and ask yourself if you really need to be receiving it. Then, do what you can to stop getting any more of it in the future.

For example, you can eliminate a lot of your junk mail. Some find it useful and enjoy receiving the various solicitations. My wife enjoys flipping through the many catalogs she receives. But if you want to reduce a lot of it, you can do so through the Direct Marketing Association (DMA). For telemarketing calls, you can sign up for the Do Not Call List, a federal program implemented by the Federal Trade Commission (FTC).

- *To eliminate junk mail,* sign up for the DMA's do-not-mail list by following the directions at the DMA site at www.the-dma.org.

- *To eliminate telemarketing calls,* sign up for the FTC's do-not-call list by following the directions at the FTC site at www.donotcall.gov.

As I said in Chapter 7 on delegation, if it's possible, get someone to screen your e-mails, memos, phone calls, and so on before they get to you so that you have to deal with only the items that really require your attention.

2. Clean Your Desk

As discussed in Chapter 8, a messy desk can easily lead to lost items and missed deadlines. It is also time-consuming going through the same pile of stuff day after day. For every item that hits your inbox or is piled on your desk, ask yourself:

- *Can it be delegated?* If it can and there's someone else who can handle it, delegate it. For you, there is a big time difference between "I do it" and "It gets done."

- *Can it be done quickly?* If it can be done in a minute or two, do it right away and be done with it. You can discharge twenty items in twenty minutes and be done with them.

- *Can I file it?* Create files for each day of the week.

Keep these files within arm's reach. If the item will take some time to complete, decide when you will get to it, put it on your to-do list for that day, and then put it in a folder designated for that day.

Keep a maximum of three or four items on your desk to handle right away.

Follow this same procedure with those e-mails in your "to be read file" and any saved voice mails.

3. Manage Your E-mails

The average businessperson receives around eighty e-mails a day, many of which are of little or no value. In fact, many of them are spam. Spam is junk e-mail, usually in the form of pitches for prescription drugs, weight-loss plans, and ways to get the attention of the opposite sex. Be wary of e-mailing spammers to opt out of future e-mail spams. Often, the reason you get the spam in the first place is that a computer randomly guessed your e-mail address. When you reply to

> **A lot of annoying paperwork can be eliminated by getting off memo distribution lists, mailing lists, and the like.**

get off this list, you identify yourself as a real e-mail address and invite even more spam.

Here's what you should do to eliminate spam and shrink your e-mail inbox.

- *Filter out spam.* Get a good filter or use a system such as Outlook that has a filter installed. Install SpamBusters or another good program that will help eliminate unwanted e-mail solicitations. Check your e-mail application's internal spam filter.

- *Get off the lists.* If you are receiving many unwanted e-mails from a particular individual, ask to be removed from his or her lists. This would include your inclusion in unwanted "cc" lists or news groups from which you don't want to receive so much e-mail. Be careful about getting off the spam lists as discussed earlier.

- *Open a separate e-mail account.* Just like getting an unlisted telephone number that you share with only those whom you want to give direct access, get a separate e-mail address that you use only for the important communications you wish to receive. For example, don't use your work email address for all your e-mail correspondence. You can open a free, separate, and personal account at Hotmail, Yahoo!, Google, or other sites.

- *Check e-mail only once or twice a day.* Many I speak with are chained to their e-mail server, monitoring incoming e-mail all the time. Maybe this is because e-mail creates its own sense of urgency, but most of the communications are not all that urgent. I let my incoming e-mails batch up and I respond to them a couple of times a day. It's a lot more effective than responding as they come in. Now, if your job requires immediate response to e-mails as they come to you, disregard this and read on.

- *Deal with it.* Like handling the paper, you don't want to get into the "shuffling blues" where you read e-mail, postpone action, save it, reread it later, and allow things to slip through the cracks. Follow the same advice set forth in step 2 to keep your e-mail inbox clean.

STREAMLINING RESPONSE TIME

Imagine that you need to get something done, but the person you're trying to reach is not picking up his or her phone. You might be a whiz at streamlining your own life, but you can't finish your task without the cooperation or response of the other party. What can you do to get them to give you the attention you need? If you're the caller, the following are a few ways to leave a message that will prompt a quick response.

- *Use an alternative to the telephone.* Let's face it: People you call are going to use the same tricks you use when you don't have time to pick up the phone. They'll avoid your call by shooting you to voice mail, so use a different mode of communication that might have a better rate of success of getting through. Fax your message or e-mail it, or even use a first-class letter. Some of the "old" methods are better than the new technology.
- *Don't spill the beans.* Want someone to call you back? Don't give him or her the entire spiel in your voice mail. Less is more. A little intrigue. Teasers.

Try:

Debbie, please give me a call. I thought about the problem you're having at work and I have a great idea about how to make your job easier.

Instead of:

Debbie, I found a new course for only $259 that will show us how to get a lot more done in less time with a lot less stress. The problem is I can't afford to buy it on my own. Would you be willing to kick in half of this and we could share the program? Let me know if you want to do this.

- *Be specific about when they should return your call.* If you want a return call, don't end with "Call me as soon as possible," "Call me soon," or "Call me when you can." These vague requests wind up in the "as soon as possible" pile that rarely gets acted on. Instead, give a specific day and time to call back. Don't give three or more choices because that will necessitate a call back from that person to confirm which date and time is best to return the call.

4. Manage Your Phone Calls

As discussed in Chapter 6, don't feel obligated to pick up the phone every time it rings. Only if you are paid to answer the phone do you need to answer it all the time. Use caller ID to see who is calling before you take the call. It may be better to let it go to voice mail.

Voice mail is a blessing and a curse for most people. On the upside, it is a way of accepting incoming phone calls at a low cost with more options than an answering machine and it's more effective at handling phone calls than before. For some businesses, it offers callers the opportunity to receive answers to their inquiries without talking to a real person. Businesses don't have to hire receptionists. It puts power in the hands of the caller's recipient.

On the downside for callers, voice mail is impersonal and gives the person you're calling an opportunity to duck your calls. You don't pick up the phone every time it rings, and neither do the people you call. Of course, when they call you back, they get your voice mail system and then you have to listen to their message and decide whether or not to return their call. Telephone tag and you're it!

If you're the recipient of a call, follow the advice in step 2 for addressing the messages in your voice mail inbox.

Take a minute to think about your paper inbox and your e-mail and voice mail inboxes. Think about how you use the various communications tools at your disposal and if your calls, e-mails, and paper correspondence usually get through or if they reside in someone else's inbox. If the latter, follow the steps in this chapter to help you be more effective. When you're in control of the medium and the message, you're in control of your life.

10

SPEEDIER READING

Tips for Reading More, Faster

———◆———

We get more words thrown at us in one day than our great-grandparents saw in a lifetime. Look around and words are everywhere: newspapers, books, faxes, Web sites, e-mails, text messages, television, billboards, and mail.

You might be surprised to discover that you spend about two hours each day reading. Think about it. From the morning paper to e-mails at work, Web pages, reports, and the novel you pick up at bedtime, a big part of your day is spent reading words on a page or screen.

The average person reads approximately 200 words a minute. What if you could double your reading speed from 200 to 400 words a minute? Then what took two hours will take one hour. Or you can spend the same amount of time reading and read twice as much. Speed reading could make you twice as efficient at absorbing information.

There are many myths about speed reading. Some people think it requires a lot of education and study. Not so. (It will, however, require a lot of practice, as does any other skill.) Others think speed reading is a skimming technique where you look at every other or third word and lose the flavor and enjoyment of your reading. Not true. You see and enjoy everything. You just learn to do it more rapidly and efficiently.

HOW TO READ FASTER

Speed-reading skills build on the way you were taught to read. You were first shown symbols that were given names. (For example, a symbol that looks like a tent with a horizontal line through it is an A.) Next, you were taught to assign phonetic sounds to each of those named symbols. So A sounds like aye, B sounds like bee, and C sounds like see. Then, if you were like most kids, you learned the alphabet with a little song to help you remember it. You remember the "ABC Song," I'm sure.

Speed reading could make you twice as efficient at absorbing information.

Then your teacher put some of those symbols and sounds together to form a word.

"C-A-T. Now, sound that out for me."

"Cah-Ahh-Tuh,"

"Oh, I get it! Cat!"

And very quickly you and millions of other kids learned that C-A-T, in that specific sequence, represented our furry friend, and no longer did you have to sound it out each time.

In your next lesson, the teacher may have expanded a word for new meaning. "Let's take *cat* and add on C and H. *Catch*. Sound that out. C-A-T-C-H. That's it! See the girl catch the ball. *Catch*, a new word. There's no cat in that anymore! And add on three more letters to *catch*, I-N-G, and you have *catching*, which is yet another concept." And so the process continued. You learned letters in a sequence, one word at a time, and built your vocabulary.

Then it was time to put some of the words together to form simple sentences.

"See the cat run."

"Watch the girl catch the ball."

You were able to put some sentences together to form paragraphs and paragraphs grew to fill pages to form whole chapters, all the while you read just one word at a time, as if there existed a stop sign between each word.

Now, what does this have to do with speed reading?

When most of us read, we see each word, sound it out in our mind, process it, and then assign meaning to it in the context of the words around it. As a result, what happens is that we tie our reading rate in with our speech rate. Most people talk and listen at the rate of 200 words a minute. The good news is that your brain is equipped to absorb information from written material at a rate up to 2,000 words a minute. The secret to speed reading is to overcome the habit of sounding out the words in your mind.

Here are several ways to teach yourself to speed read. Try one or all of them and practice every time you read.

1. Read Words and Phrases as Units

Imagine going to a concert to hear your favorite group. Instead of playing all the instruments, notes, and vocals simultaneously, imagine that the performers play the music in separate bits. Here's a chord on a guitar. Now, here is a drum roll. Next, let's hear the horns. The performance would last for weeks.

But this is the way most of us read: word by word, in bits, as if there were a stop sign between each word in a sentence. Speed reading means taking out all these stops so you can read several words at a time. It means reading letters, words, and phrases *as units*.

This is not a new skill. You already do it without thinking

about it. You already see words that take only a split second to register instant meaning. Imagine I place a flip chart before you and I quickly flip up the top page to expose five words: "The United States of America." How many times have you seen this phrase? Lots. You don't have to sound it out to understand it. You don't have to read each word one at a time. Perhaps you did the first few times you were exposed to this phrase, but now you read all five words instantly.

Here's another example of speed reading. On my way home from work, I approach my exit on the highway. The sign is posted a half mile before the exit, "Main Street Next Exit." I see that as a unit, a sequence of letters that automatically communicate to me the need to slow down and prepare to jump off the highway. I do not sound out, read, and analyze every word. I process the four words as a unit.

You do this with numbers as well. You can quickly pick out your ten-digit telephone number from a list of unfamiliar telephone numbers because your brain instantly recognizes the specific sequence of numbers for your home phone.

Speed reading is only possible with practice. The more you recognize patterns, the faster you will read. The more you read, the more you'll recognize the patterns. It's that easy.

2. Use Your Index Finger as a Pacer

To learn how to quickly read and process words as units, you need to practice by reading a lot. You start by doing it deliberately. How? First, use your index finger as a pacer, at least when you first begin to speed read.

Have you ever seen a greyhound race? The dogs are released from the gate at the sound of the bell and a mechanical rabbit mounted on a rail on the inside of the track is set to go just a little faster than the fastest dog in the pack. The dogs all run in the right direction and over the finish line. The fastest dog wins the race.

What would happen if the racetrack did not use that mechanical rabbit? The bell would sound, the gate would open, and without the rabbit to guide and coax them, the dogs would likely be running in different directions, some playing with one another and others digging holes.

Likewise, when you read your eyes tend to wander, slowing you down. Use your index finger as your mechanical

> **The more you recognize patterns, the faster you will read. The more you read, the more you'll recognize the patterns.**

rabbit. Go to the top of a page and start from left to right, line after line, reading the text as the words pass by. Go at a pace that is comfortable, where you have comprehension as you follow your finger across each line. Keep the finger moving smoothly, without stopping or going back. What will occur is you will find your eyes wanting to wander, yet your finger moves forward. Your finger will direct your attention and help you focus on the sentence you're reading. It will take a little getting used to, but practice the technique as much as you can.

Now, there will be some practical problems. For example, you probably don't want your index finger smudging up your computer screen, so for computer reading, I use the mouse and screen curser as my pacer.

Using this technique, you not only read more quickly but also your comprehension actually improves because the information is coming at you at a higher speed, engaging your brain more effectively. Also, reading pleasure increases for you because at the higher speed it is not so laborious and tedious to read. And the more you read, the more your knowledge base increases, as does your vocabulary, permitting you to read even more effectively.

3. Practice Push-up Drills

Competitive runners often put heavy weights around their ankles when they practice for a race. It is the overload principle. Come race time, they will remove those heavy weights and will feel lighter on their feet.

Baseball players use the same technique. A player is on deck, next in line for his turn at the plate, and he practices in the on-deck circle with two or more heavy bats, overloading himself. When it's his turn to bat, he uses a lighter bat.

You can take advantage of this same principle by practicing push-up drills.

First, establish your baseline. Get an easy-to-read book, perhaps a novel. Set a timer for two minutes. Practice reading for these two minutes with the goal of good comprehension. Remember, you will be using your index finger as a pacer. Get a sense of the speed you can go to maintain fairly

> **Overload your brain with twice the words you normally absorb so that when you return to reading for comprehension, your speed will naturally elevate upward.**

good comprehension. At the end of the two minutes, use a pencil to mark how far you have read. Add up the number of lines you just read. Determine how many words on average are on each line. Now multiply the average number of words (typically around ten or so) by the number of lines you read. Divide that number by two to determine how many words you can read per minute. For example, let's say you read eighty-two lines in two minutes. The average line has ten words. You read 820 words in two minutes, or 410 words per minute.

Then practice a push-up drill. Set your timer for five minutes and, using your index finger as a pacer, read at twice the speed you went when you experienced good comprehension. Don't go so fast that the words are a blur, but fast enough to create an overload of words coming at you. Practice this for the full five minutes. You will not be enjoying any real comprehension, but you are not practicing the push-up drill for comprehension. You are overloading your brain with twice the words you normally absorb so that when you return to reading for comprehension, your speed will naturally elevate upward. Push yourself.

When you complete the five-minute push-up drill, take a short break and then return to the material again and do another two-minute reading, now reading for comprehension. At the end of the two minutes, with a pencil, note how far you get. Add up the lines. Did you get any farther? Most people do. Why? Because you added the element of the push-up drill. You stretched yourself so that when you returned to reading for comprehension, your previous rate was inadequate.

Now, if you did not get any farther or even if you fell behind, don't worry. Go back and practice the push-up drill again and again. The speed will come to you.

You can use the same material to practice your push-up drills over and over. You are just using that to create an elevated flow of words to your brain, to stretch yourself and improve your reading speed. Whenever you are about to do some significant reading, prepare yourself by doing another quick push-up drill before you start your actual reading. It takes only five minutes.

Practice, practice, practice. Your speed will gradually increase. Your comprehension will go up. Reading will become more pleasurable. And you will absorb a lot more information in less time, enhancing your personal productivity along the way.

11

TAKING NOTE

WRITING EFFECTIVE NOTES

━━━◆━━━

I f you hear a message just once and don't make a note of it or review it in any way, you will probably forget 95 percent of it within the next month. If you attend a meeting, seminar, or class for three hours, you will probably retain only about nine minutes' worth of information. What a waste of time! But that is the reality of almost all the information you're exposed to only once.

Repetition is the key to effective learning. Hearing, reading, and thinking about the same piece of information over and over again solidifies your memory of it. With just a little reinforcement, you can boost your retention by 10, 15, 20 percent, or more, effectively increasing your productivity for that learning experience twice, three times, four times, and more.

To help in the process, you need to be an effective note taker and write quick notes whenever it is important for you to better retain information you encounter. This includes attending a staff meeting, consulting with your doctor at your annual physical, meeting with your boss, reading a newspaper, or attending a class, seminar, or speech. In other words, it helps to take notes almost all the time. You absorb more information in the time you have.

HOW TO TAKE EFFECTIVE NOTES

The following are some tips to help you absorb and retain the information you receive each day.

1. Use a Consistent Tool for Note Taking

Some people carry a spiral-bound notebook everywhere they go. Others prefer to use their laptops or PDAs (Palm handhelds, BlackBerries, etc.) for this purpose. If you use paper, write only on one side because writing on both sides may cause you to overlook important notes later on. Carry extra pens at all times. Preferably, use the same pad or device for all your notes. (It's difficult to keep track of notes

> Repetition is the key to effective learning. Hearing, reading, and thinking about the same piece of information over and over again solidifies your memory of it.

that are stored in many different places, i.e., one for meet-ings, one for lectures, etc.) You can categorize your notes within your note-taking system.

2. Be Selective in What You Write Down

You do not need to take all the information down verbatim. Your task is not to be a court stenographer, taking down all the testimony word for word. Write down the major points and then the subpoints that relate to the major point. Don't write down (or type) everything word for word. Don't copy the projection verbatim. Pay attention to anything the speaker repeats. The most important information is said more than once and in more than one way.

If it is crucial for you to remember lots of detail, bring a tape recorder and tape the entire presentation while you take notes. Later on, you can relisten to the recording for reinforcement and to pick up additional detail.

3. Use Abbreviations and Symbols

You'll never be able to write down every word or idea you hear, and you shouldn't. Instead, develop your own short-hand for frequently used terms, especially if you're hand-writing them as opposed to typing them. As a law student, I used K for *contract*, D for *defendant*, P for *plaintiff*, w/o for *without*, w/ for *with*, and $ for *money*. (That should be easy to remember!) Whenever you run across an often-used phrase, abbreviate it. In my case BRD was quicker to write than *beyond a reasonable doubt*. And I used initials for full names: JFK for *John Fitzgerald Kennedy*. To shorten names of people familiar to you, use just the first initial, such as B for *Bradford* or A for *Adrian*.

Other common abbreviations and symbols include:

+-*plus or and*
eg-*example*
US-*United States*
←-*left*
→-*right or results in*
2-*to*
4-*for*
w/-*with*
w/o-*without*
vs-*versus*
*-*crucial*
#-*number*
@-*at*
&-*and*
=-*equals*
~-*approximately*

esp-*especially*
info-*information*
msg-*message*
mtg-*meeting*

Some people use the entire first syllable of a word and then tack on the first letter of the second syllable, e.g., ind for *individual*. Others omit vowels, e.g., prblem for *problem* or vcblry for *vocabulary* or yr for *your*. Just keep the *g* of words that end with "ing," like climbg for *climbing*, ckg for *checking*, fstng for *fastening*. Leave out unimportant verbs and nouns such as *was, there, is, a,* and *the.*

Develop your own symbols and abbreviations and your note taking will be a whole lot easier.

You can apply the same techniques for note taking for your reading. If the book or newspaper I'm reading is my own, I write the notes in the margins of the book as I read. I won't keep that newspaper and the notes I made, but the simple exercise of making notes about an important story does a lot for my retention. Sometimes, I will transfer those notes to my notebook to ensure that I'll remember them.

Occasionally, I use a yellow highlighter as a substitute for note taking in a book. I don't use it that much, however, because highlighting something is not nearly as effective for retention as writing my own words describing the point.

Highlighting can be useful in moderation when you highlight the important points only. I have seen students highlight entire chapters line for line, word for word. That is almost always overkill, as you need not remember every word. Don't let your highlighting become an art exercise.

4. Draw Diagrams

Let's say you attend a seminar on marketing. You write across the top of your page "Marketing Seminar" and underline it. As major points are established under that heading, you draw diagonal lines under the main topic and write in the major topics. They might include budgeting, sales training, and specific programs. As major topics are developed under each of these subheadings, draw diagonal lines under that specific subtopic and add in the additional detail. A flow chart or hierarchical diagram can be a lot less work than scripting out written notes and just as effective (or more so) for the recall.

You'll never be able to write down every word or idea you hear, and you shouldn't.

If you're a visual person, it might help you to draw simple illustrations to represent an idea. If the speaker is talking about, for example, what happens during a heart attack, you might want to sketch a quick diagram of the heart and arteries and draw arrows and labels to represent what the speaker is saying.

5. Label Your Notes

Before or after you take your notes, be sure to properly label and file them by placing subject and date on the top, as you are unlikely, when time has passed, to remember accurately later on. "Are these from Tuesday's meeting or Friday's?"

6. Review Your Notes

Make it a point to set aside time immediately after the event to review your notes, the sooner the better. To permanently retain the information, you need to review your notes multiple times. The more repetition, the higher the recall.

7. Write Clearly

If you're writing your notes by hand, be sure to write legibly. Sometimes, when I get excited about what I am listening to

I start scribbling fast and carelessly, so that when it comes time to review my notes, my handwriting is too sloppy to be legible.

＊

Your ability to retain information is crucial if you want to lead a more efficient life. Use your notes as a prosthesis, an extension of your memory. With good note-taking skills and careful review of your notes, you'll see that much of what you write will find its way into your permanent memory and be translated into your actions.

> **Set aside time immediately after the event to review your notes, the sooner the better.**

12

THE MEMORY OF AN ELEPHANT

Improving Your Memory

———◆———

O ne evening back in college I remember sharing a quantity of beer with a friend in my dorm room. In the course of our conversation, he declared, "I don't have a good memory. I cannot remember important things. Even when I study, when it comes exam time, I come up empty."

Believing that you can have untrained memories but not bad memories, I replied, "If you have a bad memory, if you cannot retain important information, then I want you to forget the word *elephant*."

"What? Forget the word *elephant*? How can I do that?"

"Don't remember it. Forget it. Don't memorize it. *Elephant*. You know, that huge gray animal with the long trunk with an affinity for peanuts and a healthy fear of mice. Rammmph, rammmph, rammmph," I screamed with my nose to my shoulder and my arm waving from left to right, like the trunk of the elephant. I was loud, my display was physical, and it was all exaggerated.

"Now what animal are you going to forget that we talked about?"

"Elephant," my friend replied.

"Now forget it, please," I said.

Throughout the rest of that semester, whenever I would see my friend he would shout, "Elephant!" He never forgot it because we repeated it so often. It was reinforced with repetition and his memory of it was secured. (Many years have passed since I was with my friend, but if I ran into him today I would bet his first word to me would be *elephant*!)

Many people believe they do not have a good memory. I don't think so. As my elephant story suggests, memories can be made by applying significance to a fact or event and repeating it over and over again. Assuming there's no physical limitation that would impair memory, there's no such thing as a bad memory. But there is an untrained memory and an underutilized and lazy memory—nothing you can't fix.

> **Memories can be made by applying significance to a fact or event and repeating it over and over again.**

STRENGTHEN YOUR MEMORY

It's a given that a good memory will help your productivity in countless ways. The following are a few steps that I find essential to training an active memory.

1. Memory by Repetition

News stories we hear about only once are easily forgotten because their essence was not memorized in the first place. These occupy only our current attention span. Try this: Videotape a newscast for half an hour, then watch it as you normally would with your usual level of attention. See if your thoughts wander from time to time. Then, one week later, give yourself a test. Put to writing all you remember about what you watched the week before on that videotape. Then rewatch the tape and see how much you missed. You may have missed much detail in the stories and even some whole stories as well.

Now compare this experience with a news story that you heard many times over. For example, do you remember where you were when you first heard about the terrorist attacks on the morning of September 11, 2001? I am sure you do, and you probably recall much detail about that terrible day because through the news media you saw and heard the many details over and over again.

Even when you are not paying particular attention, you are memorizing simply through repetition. Can you fill in the blank? "You deserve a _____ today." Did you guess *break*? Did this remind you of McDonald's? Even though it hasn't used this slogan for years, you most likely have it memorized because you were probably one of the millions who had that slogan repeated to you hundreds and thousands of times. "Have you driven a _____ lately?" (Ford.) And for some of my older readers, "Winston tastes good like a _____ should." (Cigarette, remember?)

Nothing works as well as simple rote to improve memory. If you need to memorize ritual, long passages of text, a poem, or the "Gettysburg Address" for school, then practice the piece over and over until you have it memorized.

2. Memory by Visualization

Put the facts you need to memorize into pictures using all your senses. Pretend that you have to memorize some information about a key battle from history. See the battle in your mind's eye and in great detail. See the 10,000 soldiers, the weapons they carry, the ground they walk on, and the half mile they cover. See the color of their uniforms and the condition of the sky in your mind. Smell what was probably in the air at the time. Hear the loud sounds of gunfire and the whistle of artillery. Taste the air hanging heavy over the battlefield. Feel the clods of dirt being tossed in the air from nearby explosions and pelting your back and arms. Then mix that with emotion as you read the facts. Feel sadness, disgust, or fear. Emotion will be the glue to make these facts stick with you.

Studies show that you can also significantly improve your sports performance in tennis, racquetball, golf, and the like by visualizing the technique, which commits it to memory. You first learn the mechanical steps to improved performance and then use all five senses to master the technique perfectly, over and over and experiencing strong emotions, all the while solidifying the memory that will later communicate better instructions to your muscles to enhance your performance.

I applied this to improve my racquetball game. I watched a videotape of a person on a racquetball court delivering a perfect serve of the ball over and over for ten minutes a day followed by ten minutes of seeing myself in the same mode, hitting that ball perfectly, serve after serve, while experiencing the joy of victory in my performance. To my delight and surprise, in no time I significantly improved my service and game results because I was truly memorizing the proper technique and then applying it to increase my success.

The more you involve the senses and emotions in the process of memorizing, the more you use both sides of your brain. This shortens the time needed to master the information and, better yet, solidifying the memory, banking that valuable information you will now be able to draw on from time to time to improve your personal productivity.

3. Memory by Association

Your chances of remembering something are much better if you can relate the new information to something you already know.

Say you want to memorize the names of the Great Lakes. They are Huron, Ontario, Michigan, Erie, and Superior. As names of lakes alone, it may be difficult for you to retain and be able to recite all five. However, take the first letter of each lake, H-O-M-E-S, and you get *homes*. Remember *homes* to trigger your memory of the five Great Lakes.

> **The more you involve the senses and emotions in the process of memorizing, the more you use both sides of your brain.**

"What if I can't recall *homes* when I need to recall the five Great Lakes?" Try linking the key word to something or someplace you know intimately, inside and out. For example, see your home. Walk through the first five rooms of your home in your mind's eye and see one of the Great Lakes sloshing around in a fish tank in each of those five rooms. Connect the name of the lake to each room. It's a nutty vision, but the more exaggerated you make the vision, the better it will help you to access these memory connections.

4. Make Up Rhymes and Phrases

Everyone likes rhymes, which is great, because they are a great device for improving your memory. "Fall back and spring forward" helps you remember which way to adjust the clock before and after daylight savings time. Want to remember historical dates? How about, "Columbus sailed the ocean blue in 1492"? Days in each month? "Thirty days hath September, April, June, and November. All the rest have thirty-one except February." When did the first astronaut set foot on the moon? "The moon sure looked fine in 1969." Someone's age? "Uncle Sid who's poor was born in 1944." You get the idea. Make up your own.

5. Stay in Good Health

Good memory starts with good health. Get enough sleep. Eat right. Stay away from mind-altering chemicals. Exercise and breathe right, getting a lot of oxygen to your brain. And keep your stress level down. Stress impairs memory.

6. Have Good Prostheses

Having a good day planner, notebook, or PDA is a great memory improver, too. Record appointments and things you have to do in yours so that you free up your mind for memorizing those bigger items. Put in your dentist appointment, staff meetings, and social commitments. Put down projects you have to do, phone calls you need to make, and other tasks in that day planner and use it as an extension of your brain. Add in important dates such as birthdays and anniversaries.

Seeing these items over and over again as you look ahead on your calendar or to-do lists will help remind you of them.

> **Your chances of remembering something are much better if you can relate the new information to something you already know.**

Oh, and don't forget where you placed your day planner, notebook, or PDA.

———◆———

Now let's test your memory: What was the word my friend was to forget?

13

WHATSHISNAME?

THE SCIENCE OF REMEMBERING NAMES

◆——◆——◆

I used to be terrible at remembering names. This bad habit became embarrassingly obvious when I was teaching undergraduates at Mercy College in New York. I had four classes a semester with about thirty students each. The faculty were required to call the names on the roster at the beginning of each class as a way of taking attendance.

At the beginning of each class, I was eager to get into the day's material and share my gems of wisdom with a room full of bright minds, so I would rush through the roster. I called the names, and when I heard "here," I checked each student's name without looking up to associate his or her name with his or her face. The result was that I rarely got to know my students by name. I could recognize their faces but not their names. At the end of the semester, I might know six or seven by their names and the rest would have nicknames: "Hey sport. Hi kiddo. How's my star student today?"

You may question what name remembering has to do with productivity. The answer is that remembering names makes you a more important communicator, which makes you more effective and productive. Being able to call a person by name elevates the rapport you have with that person, increasing the level of trust. Not being able to recall a name can be devastating to your potential social or business opportunity when it is assumed and expected that you should know this person's name.

Realizing this, I have come a long way since my days as a college professor. If I start a three-day seminar with a group of fifty people, within the first hour and a half I make a point of knowing everyone by name. When I see them return the next morning without their name tags, I can welcome them back by name. It is impressive because it means a lot to be recognized. "He must really take an interest in me," they conclude.

HOW TO REMEMBER NAMES

These tips will help you effectively remember the names of people you meet. Many of these are based on the advice in Chapter 12, but applied specifically to remembering names.

1. Repeat Names Frequently in a Short Time Span

If you have the opportunity to know the name of a person before you meet him or her, repeat it out loud several times. Before I leave my office for a seminar, I review the roster of people I am about to meet, reading and speaking each name slowly, learning what I can from just the names. Perhaps I know someone by the same name. Maybe I have heard of that person before. I especially spend time getting the correct pronunciation of unfamiliar names.

With the roster fresh in my mind, I arrive at the seminar. People start to arrive and I meet each person one on one and introduce myself and get his or her name. If I don't quite catch it, I will ask the person to repeat it. Make a fuss over his or her name. He or she will love it.

I then see in my mind's eye that name that I also saw on my roster. I look up that name on the roster, read it, check

> **Not being able to recall a name can be devastating to your potential social or business opportunity, limiting your personal productivity.**

it off, and invite that person to the signup table to make out his or her name tag. I note the person's name again as I look at the name tag. (By the way, most people place these name tags on the left side of their chest because they are right handed and the name tag in the right hand just naturally slaps over to the left side of the chest. The next time you wear a name tag, place it on the right side of your chest. It will be more directly in the line of sight for people as they step toward you to greet you and will be more noticeable and readable. And because most put their name tags on the left side, yours being on the right side will make you stand out and draw more attention. A small detail, but remember that small changes leverage into large results.)

When I'm introduced to people, I listen to them recite their own names as they introduce themselves. I then try to ask for a little information about them. In my seminars, I call on every person by name during that exercise for some comment or contribution, seeing their name tag again before saying their name. "What do you think about that point, Sandra?" "Bruce, is this something you'd like to know more about?" By the end of this hour and a half, I have gone through at least ten repetitions of everyone's name and the recall is almost perfect, fifty names remembered.

This intentional process of concentrated repetition is powerful even outside a formal setting. For example, my wife and I spent a week vacationing at a Club Med resort in Cancun, Mexico, where we met about 200 other people. When we arrived on Saturday, I made a commitment to myself that by the end of our week together, I would know every one of the 200 guests' first names. No one was wearing a name tag, so remembering names took some extra effort. Applying the exercise of intentional and rapid repetition, by Wednesday of that week, in just five days, I knew almost everyone's first name. (The ones I did not get to know were those I couldn't corner for a moment of two.)

It was hard work and I did it to prove to myself that I could do it. You can too.

2. Associate People's Names with Things You Know

As you learn someone's name, associate it with something that will trigger his or her name when you meet again. Is Ted tall? "Tall Ted." Is Mary married? When you see her wedding ring again, you will think, "Married Mary." Does he or she remind you of a famous person? Mention this to him or her and it will reinforce your recall. Make a rhyme out of the person's name and create a nickname that will aid your recall later on. "Dan, Dan, I'm your fan." "Wendy, you're trendy."

Associate the person's name with his or her occupation. "Hi Connie, the real estate pro." "So you're Len, the engineer."

3. Visualize Their Names

If possible, break the person's name up to create a picture in your mind for recall. For Rachel, I see Ray Charles the singer shivering; "Ray" "Chill," got it? For Mr. Johnson, I might see "Jon, my son." And if his first name is Bill, I will see him giving an invoice to my son, Jon. When I meet Courtney, I am on my "knee in the court."

(Now be careful here of unintended consequences. Perhaps you meet Hamilton Frye and you see "ham being fried" but then the next time you meet Hamilton, you get your signals mixed up and you address him as "Mr. Bacon." That could be embarrassing.)

Another tactic is to imagine the person's name written on his or her forehead. You can also try to discreetly write his or her name in the air with slight movements of your index finger. Some people are wired to remember things better if they write them down.

4. Ask for a Business Card

Use the name of a person you just met as often as is practical in your initial time together and when you part, ask for his or her business card, if you don't already have it. If no card, write his or her name down and later, when you can, review those cards and notes and add the name to your database of contacts (read more about this in Chapter 21).

IF ALL ELSE FAILS

So what if this fails you (and sometimes it will)? You are not going to be able to remember every name every time. This is especially true if you meet the person again outside of context; for example, you met someone once at a business meeting and then you run into him or her at the shopping mall.

Take the initiative and move into "intro mode." You see this person at the shopping mall, you cannot think of his or her name so you approach him or her rapidly with your hand out, saying, "Hi, Don Wetmore [use your name here, please]. How have you been?" Ninety percent of the time the per-

> **As you learn someone's name, associate it with something that will trigger his or her name when you meet again.**

son's response will be, "Yes, of course, Don. Margaret Burns. I have been fine, and you?" Then just nod approvingly like you already had the person's name on the tip of your tongue and he or she got it right.

Or have a friend who doesn't know this person help you. He or she would approach this person and introduce him- or herself first to get that person's name.

And when all else fails, honesty prevails! Confess. They won't hate you. "I'm sorry, I'm having one of those blocks. What is your name again?" Then repetition, repetition, repetition. Cement that name in your brain so that you are not in the same awkward situation again.

14

THE ART OF OBSERVATION

Fine-Tuning Your Senses

O ur ability to make observations and see patterns in things once kept our ancestors alive in an environment where tigers and other enemies threatened to eat them. Today, the tigers are in cages and your enemies are likely to be a bit more civil, but the same observation skills keep you safe when crossing the street or driving a car. Perception is also an important productivity skill.

Using all your senses, that is, learning from what you see, hear, smell, feel, and taste, will help you to get more of what you want in less time. Being aware of even the most mundane activities can help improve your success. Look for the ripples in the water to see where the fish are. Watch for changes in the sky to anticipate changes in your weather. Observe how successful people, whom you may admire, use their time as a model for your own success path. In relationships or your job, take note of signals that indicate you may be headed for difficult and costly times.

Your personal productivity is not measured simply by what you are doing. If what you are doing is not getting you to where you want to go, your time is not being spent productively. Productivity is measured by what is produced from your performance. Your ability to observe this big picture helps you to focus not only on what you are doing but also what else you *could be doing better.*

SEEING IT ALL

How does observation translate into productivity? Here's a personal example. I work on a laptop. I write articles, develop spreadsheets, and update my database about as fast and as efficiently as anyone I know. In the first six months I owned the laptop, I loaded it with an incredible amount of data, pounding away at the keyboard like it was a fine piano. On a scale of 1 to 10, I would have rated my productivity as a 9 or 10. I was a superachiever.

Well, except for one small detail. I didn't back up my work. I didn't notice all that data on my hard drive, sitting there unprotected and at risk of vanishing if my hard drive died. Sure enough, the hard drive on the laptop crashed, burned, and died and I lost everything I had put onto it for the previous six months. I was like a squirrel gathering nuts for the long winter, doing it faster and better than my fellow squirrels, all the while oblivious of the raccoon that aimed to steal the fruits of my labor. If I were more observant and attentive, my cache would still be there.

Now, what was my productivity for those six months on a scale of 1 to 10? Zero. Zilch. Looking back, my efficiency at creating the data was a 9 or 10 but by neglecting the simple backup process, my performance was actually a 0, as if I had not done it at all.

The following are some other common-sense reminders of ways in which you can be more observant and, therefore, more productive.

1. Be Observant of Your Surroundings

I travel a lot in my car. While driving, I intentionally notice landmarks along the way. "Look, there's a cemetery. What an unusual bridge." Simple, but it is a great help to find my way back without wasting time getting lost or, heaven forbid, being forced to take the time to ask someone for directions!

> **Using all your senses, that is, learning from what you see, hear, smell, feel, and taste, will help you to get more of what you want in less time.**

The ability to see your context will also help you at work or home. Most of us spend hours looking for something we have lost. Over the course of a year, there's a good chance that you spent two hundred or more hours searching for missing keys, earrings, glasses, papers, and other items that you misplaced. If you had been more observant of your surroundings, you would have had much more time for more interesting and fulfilling pursuits.

2. Be Observant of Your Appearance

Are your shoelaces untied? If they are and you don't notice this and tie them, you might trip and fall. You could face many medical bills, lose work, and waste time recovering from an injury that you created because you were not practicing the art of observation. Being ignorant of your appearance may harm you in other ways, too. You may be an outstandingly productive employee, but you might not get the promotion you're seeking because you show up to work every day with your hair greasy and your fly unzipped. On the flip side, an immaculate appearance might help you progress in your career and give others a good impression of you—terrific pluses for your productivity in the scheme of things.

3. Be Observant of Your Relationships

As an attorney, I have handled more than 200 divorces, representing an equal number of men and women. On many occasions, when I would take on a new divorce case, my client, who may have recently been served with divorce papers, would lament, "This came out of the blue. I did not see this coming." That's true—my client probably did not see it coming. But he or she could have. In most cases, had my client been more tuned in to the relationship, using his or her skills of observation, he or she might have seen it coming because relationship problems begin by sending out clues far in advance of the ultimate breakup, such as increased tension or a complete lack of communciation. By being more observant of your relationships, you can potentially head off a crisis that will no doubt undermine your productivity.

4. Be Observant of the People You Admire

If you admire how someone does something, observe how

> **You may be an outstandingly productive employee, but you might not get your promotion because you show up to work every day with your hair greasy and your fly unzipped.**

they do it and apply it to your own circumstances. If you would like to improve your game of golf, watch those whom you deem to be better golfers play. If you want to improve your public speaking skills, watch excellent public speakers. If you want to dress better, observe the people who have a great sense of style. If you want to lose weight or quit smoking, watch the people who have successfully taken off pounds and quit bad habits. How are they spending their time to achieve what you are hoping to achieve? What steps are they taking to get there? How do they carry themselves and relate to others? Watch, observe, and learn. The lion cub learns to hunt efficiently by watching its mother accomplish this task. The cub doesn't go to class. It just observes and learns.

5. Be Observant of How You Interact with Others

Your productivity depends on the cooperation of other people. Relationships begin by establishing rapport with others, and you achieve this through the practice of matching and mirroring. When you meet someone for the first time and it is your goal to establish a relationship with this person, observe all of what he or she is doing physically and then match as many of those characteristics as you can. Is he or she speaking loudly or softly? You do the same. Is he or she sitting or standing? Legs crossed or both feet on the floor? Hands folded or arms crossed? Using gestures or not? Does he or she speak fast or slow? You do the same. You match it all.

Practicing this hundreds of times over the years, I have learned that it is not evident to this new person what you are doing. It is just a subtle way of being like him or her, finding commonality. You will accelerate the process when you match and mirror the physical characteristics of this new person because as he or she watches and hears you, his or her unconscious mind is saying, "This person is just like me." (See Chapter 22 for more on small talk.)

Bravo for noticing this line at the end of the chapter. Pay attention and be more observant. The world is always teaching you something.

> **If you admire how someone does something, observe how they do it and apply it to your own circumstances.**

15

THE IDEA TIME CAPSULE

CAPTURING YOUR EUREKA MOMENTS

You are exposed to a torrent of great ideas every time you listen to others, read a book, newspaper, or magazine, or surf the Internet. Your brain is always weaving miscellaneous threads of information into creative ideas. For many of us, however, these great ideas are never acted on because we do not have a simple system to capture them. Our greatest ideas often come to us unexpectedly and then they vanish.

Your capture device is simple. Use an idea notebook. I like to use a spiral-bound notepad. You may find using your PDA will do the job. It may be the same planner in which you have your calendar, to-do list, and notepad. Set up your own system and have it readily accessible. As you come across a great new idea to improve your life, record it. Think of your system as a time capsule. It's as simple as that. The hard part is remembering to do it.

THE IDEA

Think of your idea notebook as a storage space where you keep seeds for future harvest. Keep your notebook on hand when you're surfing the Web or going to a meeting. These ideas may also come to you at the strangest times: during your commute, in the middle of the night, or at the ball-game. Perhaps it's your subconscious working when you are at rest. In any case, your idea notebook should always be within arm's reach.

What are some examples of the great ideas that might come to you?

- *New business concepts you may one day implement*
- *Ways of being a better parent*
- *Observations on how to be a better public speaker*
- *Ideas about how to make some extra money on the side*
- *Languages you want to learn*
- *Ways to preserve the memory of your parents by videotaping them or making a scrapbook*

Our greatest ideas often come to us unexpectedly, and then they vanish.

- *The plot of a novel you want to write*
- *Ways to remodel your kitchen*

Ultimately, your notebook will accumulate more ideas than you could ever achieve in a lifetime. In fact, your list guarantees that you will never run out of meaningful goals to pursue in your life. It eliminates the chance of arriving at the point of "Now I've accomplished all that, what do I do next? My goal bucket went dry."

Review your notebook from time to time. It may occur to you that developing just one skill area could significantly enhance the other vital areas of your life: health, family, financial, intellectual, social, professional, and spiritual. Perhaps overcoming your shyness about public speaking would improve your mental health, your earning potential, and your social life all at the same time.

Many great ideas, while "great," are not timely. The notebook is a placeholder so that when the time and place are more appropriate, the concept is there waiting for you. Time helps your idea notebook to become a laboratory of creative experiments with the best of the bunch bubbling to the top of the priority list for action and incorporation into your life. If you hadn't written your idea down, you would have abandoned it. This is true productivity, thoughtfully channeling your resources to the best use at the best time.

For example, I have money-making ideas from twenty years ago (I have had my notebook for a long time!) that today make sense and fit into my life, whereas twenty years ago they did not. The ideas have been there in my warehouse all that time, as assets waiting to be exploited.

———◆———

Over time, your notebook will become a written history of your priorities. Earlier in my life, many of the ideas I captured were about ways to make money. That makes sense. I was younger with a wife and little kids to support, so it drove my priorities toward the financial arena. Today, my idea notebook contains great ideas about relationships and intellectual development.

> **The notebook is a placeholder so that when the time and place for your idea are appropriate, the great idea is there waiting for you.**
>
> ———◆———

16

SCRAPS OF YOUR LIFE

RECORDING SUCCESS WITH DIARIES, PICTURES, AND OTHER MEDIA

———◆———

Most people seem to be better at recalling the bad things in life than their achievements. Saddled with the psychic baggage of their failures, these people often believe that they can't do things and have never been able to do things. They forget the good grades, the graduations, the first dates, the vacations, the promotions, and the thank-yous from people they've helped. Reminders of the good things provide momentum. They boost your self-confidence and help you produce more good things in your life. For this reason, it's a good idea to preserve a record of your achievements with diaries, pictures, and other media.

As I've mentioned before, productivity transcends simply working faster. It means being more effective in your everyday life, maintaining a balance, and having a long-term vision that extends deep into the past and reaches toward the future. As the days become years and the years become a lifetime, your productivity is measured by how close you have come to achieving your goals. Your diary will help you to record and build on your past successes.

PRESERVE YOUR SUCCESS

A diary will help you record your progress and pitfalls so that you can learn from them in the future. Your diary is not a chore, nor does it have to be a time-consuming practice. Even a couple minutes of scribblings each day will make a difference in the future.

There are three diary formats. Find one that suits your personal style and that would be easy for you to do regularly.

1. The Traditional Narrative Diary

A traditional diary, an account of the day's events, is written longhand in a journal or typed out on a computer. It captures not only specific events and achievements but also reflects your emotional state at the time you wrote it.

It might appear as follows:

> **Reminders of the good things provide momentum. They boost your self-confidence and help produce more good things in your life.**

Thursday, November 4
Dear Diary:

What a day! I arrived at the office at 9 and had a voice mail waiting for me. It was John, the boss, and he wanted to see me as soon as I got in to discuss something of "great importance." My initial reaction was fear. I have been working hard all year, but I did drop the ball a couple of times.

I went directly to John's office. He looked grim and asked me to sit down. He started by asking me, "Do you really like working here?" My heart sank. This was it. The ax was about to fall.

"I sure do," I said.

"Well, we like having you here, too, and I think you have been underutilized and underpaid. If you will accept it, we'd like to promote you to department head with a 15 percent salary increase effective today. Would that be okay?"

Would that be okay? I almost jumped out of my skin! "Yes! I'll take it!"

As soon as I returned to my desk, everyone in the department came by to congratulate me. They even set up a surprise luncheon on my behalf. And when I got home tonight, Nancy had a surprise gathering of our neighbors with cake and balloons to celebrate my good fortune.

You get the idea. You can make your daily account as descriptive as you choose, the more the better. You will never regret long accounts in the years ahead. In fact, I was recently reviewing some old diary entries I made some thirty years ago and I wish now that I had taken an extra few minutes with each entry to record more information.

Your diary should certainly include your successes, but record your disappointments as well. Looking back, you can find patterns in your own behavior. With effort, being conscious of your foibles will help you correct yourself in the future.

2. The Chronological Diary

A second diary method is brief but captures important events in your life chronologically. They serve as memory triggers.

January 1: New Year's party at Williamson's
January 12: Attended theater—saw *Cats*
January 18: Took delivery of new car: Toyota
February 1: Attended Jen's recital
February 10: Got promotion

You add the next entries as important milestones are achieved.

3. The Detailed Chronology

A final way to diary your success is similar to the chronological method but it is done daily and with more depth using the seven vital areas: health, family, financial, intellectual, social, professional, and spiritual. You may find it useful to use your day planner or PDA for this. Every night in daily planning put a key word or a short phrase beside each of your seven vital areas, highlighting something positive that you experienced in each area.

It might appear as follows:

Health: Lost one and a half pounds
Family: Homework with kids
Financial: Paid bills
Intellectual: Read for an hour
Social: Lunch with Karen
Professional: Finished A items on to-do list
Spiritual: Meditated this morning

To save time, you might abbreviate these seven areas rather than writing them out in full each day: H, F, F, I, S, P, and S.

Most of the entries will be minor victories rather than major accomplishments, but little victories, when strung together, form patterns of greater victories as time goes by. This exercise also causes you to be more conscious of attending to your life balance, which, as I've said over and over again, is the real key to productivity.

<hr>

When you are feeling a little down or when success has eluded you for some time and your productivity is suffering, go back and review your entries from a month ago, a year ago, and a decade ago and see the totality of the successes you have enjoyed. Relive the emotions of those great moments and get yourself back on track, charged up, and more productive. This will serve as a great centering device and morale booster.

YOUR MULTIMEDIA RECORD

There is more than one way to record the passing of time and the accumulation of life achievements. Besides your text record, consider using other media such as photos, video, and audio to create a multimedia record.

As a kid, I took an interest in photography. Using my black-and-white Brownie camera, I photographed my pet rabbits, friends, and family events. I then spent most of my weekly allowance having the rolls of film processed at the local drugstore. In my teen years, I got more interested in photography and built a darkroom in my basement and

> **Keeping a journal causes you to be more conscious of attending to your life balance, which is the real key to productivity.**

processed my own pictures. I have created a number of photo albums over the years that I review from time to time to more clearly recall my past.

Later, I got into color prints and then slides. Nothing fancy, all amateur stuff, but it held the memories of my past and the visions of friends and relatives who have passed on, images impossible to create today. I later got into making home movies and then bought a VCR camera.

The point is, we now have closets filled with pictures, photo albums, movies reels, and VCR tapes documenting memories of my past. We share these prints and copies liberally with friends and family. For example, as each child gets engaged, my wife, Nancy, prepares an extensive album of pictures that are relevant to that child's life. It is a thick album and a wonderful gift but is only possible because we took lots of pictures over the years to capture their moments.

Today, you can get a good-quality digital camera for around $100 and take as many pictures as you want and then download them to your computer without having to spend a ton of money on film and processing. You can send selected shots around the world for free via e-mail, sharing your photos with friends and family. You can do the same with a digital or video camera by plugging it into your television and sharing memories with others.

Make it a point to get a tape recorder and record interviews with important people in your life, preserving their voice on tape.

For example, I did this years ago with my grandmother. One evening I sat down with her and my old reel-to-reel tape recorder and recorded several hours of her recollections of important events in her life. It was fun for both of us. Some ten years after she passed on, I came across the tape and had copies made for my grandmother's children—my father, my uncle, and my two aunts—and presented the copies to each one that Christmas. To them, it was like a gift of a million dollars to be able to hear their mother's voice again.

I could not have done that without an intentional effort of looking ahead to the future, knowing that the present would quickly pass and that what I do now will make a difference later.

←——◆◆——→

Be sure to schedule time to make a record in your diaries and on film and recordings and to review these records from time to time in the future. Remember, productivity requires building on past experiences for future success.

Your personal productivity
is improved when you can
competently and confidently
communicate with others.
In this section, you will learn
important techniques to improve your
oral and written communication skills.
You'll also learn ways to expand your
network of connections, bearing in
my mind that one of your strongest
productivity assets is people.

PART 3 COMMUNICATION

17

WRITE RIGHT

Tips for Better Written Communications

We are all writers. Throughout your life you write e-mails, letters, résumés, reports, proposals, instant messages, business plans, meeting minutes, diaries, memos, and executive briefings. You might also write trip reports, outlines, class notes, poetry, Web sites, the Christmas card annual summary of what your family did this year, thank-you notes, and even a book one day. Your personal productivity is directly affected by your ability to competently and confidently express yourself in your writing. The better you write, the more efficiently and effectively you communicate your ideas to get the results you want, whether it be a raise, a new business proposal, or a customer service complaint. Of course, many of the exercises in this book are also writing related, including daily planning, diaries, and logs.

That said, writing has changed over the years. Few of us take the time to send letters to friends and relatives to stay in touch. Telephone calls have become so inexpensive that it is more convenient to call than to write. Attention spans have decreased as well. In this harried world, few of us have the time to read long writings to get to the information we need. That's why, when you do write, you need to be effective.

STRENGTHEN YOUR WRITING SKILLS NOW

I cannot offer a full course on writing skills in this one chapter. Instead, I will share a number of useful tips to help you improve your writing. Remember, like speed reading or public speaking skills, this will require an investment of time. Here's how to get started.

1. Enroll in a Writing Class

If you are seriously deficient in basic writing skills, fix them.

> **The better you write, the more efficiently and effectively you communicate your ideas to get the results you want.**

You need not be a prisoner of your past. There are a number of writing skills classes and seminars available for you today. Check your local adult education programs and colleges for writing skills classes. You may be able to find a class in your area through an Internet search. Enroll in a writing class and develop your skills.

2. Practice, Practice, Practice

We've all been told that repetition is the key to any skill we wish to develop and improve. Write often. Write every day. Write in your personal diary. Write a letter to an elected official about your opinion on an issue you feel strongly about. It is good writing practice and your letters could make a difference. (Politicians do pay attention to these letters.) The more you write, the better you get. Also, read more. The more you read, the better you'll write.

3. Improve Your Vocabulary

When you come across a word you do not understand, look it up. I carry a list in my day planner with the heading "Words to Look Up." Whenever I come across an unfamiliar word, I write it on the list and look up the definition later. Have a good thesaurus nearby to find and use different words to express the same thoughts and expand your vocabulary even more. Do crossword puzzles. It's a great way to relax while exercising the brain and building up your vocabulary.

GET THE BEST RESULTS WHEN
YOU WRITE FOR OTHERS

Besides strengthening your general writing skills, remember that you are writing to communicate. You want your writing to be as effective as possible when you're conveying an idea, directing a course of action, or motivating someone to do something. Your competence here adds a lot to your bottom-line productivity. The following are some tips on how to write when you want to persuade someone or get his or her attention in a positive way.

1. Write in a Positive Tone for Positive Results

When writing to get others to do something for you, make sure to write in a positive tone. Avoid negative language if you can. The following are two examples of a memo to your fellow workers wherein you want them to do a better job of keeping the office kitchen cleaner:

a. *"The kitchen area is a mess because some of us are sloppy. Clean up your mess!"*

b. *"When the kitchen area is clean, we all benefit. Thank you for cleaning up after you use it! It helps us all."*

Which one is more effective for you? Probably the second, positive, encouraging example.

Which do you prefer?

a. *"No smoking."*

b. *"Thank you for not smoking."*

Both convey the same message (don't smoke here) but the second, positive version is more effective.

2. Use *You* Rather than *I*

The number-one topic of conversation most people have is themselves. Write about what the other person will learn, benefit from, gain, and improve from reading what you have written rather than about what *you* have learned, benefited, gained, and improved. The *I* experience is instructive, but the *you* message brings you, the reader, in more effectively.

3. Use Active Words over Passive Words

Active words are powerful verbs and adjectives that create pictures of action and are more effective than passive words.

a. *Our sales were higher and were a record for our team this quarter.*

b. *Our team sold more and broke our record this quarter.*

The second sentence is active and alive with energy, while the first is passive, a flat statement of fact. Both communicate the same information. The active sentence structure does it with more zest.

4. Use Peoples' Names Whenever Possible

If you are writing a proposal to Dave Jones, address him personally. Avoid "To Whom It May Concern" or "Dear Sir or Madam." Before you write a complaint to the electronics company, do some research. Find a person's name that your letter can be directed to. If appropriate, use first names. "Dear Dave" grabs the reader's attention and interest better than "Dear Mr. Jones." If possible, use Dave's name in the body of your writing. "As you review our proposal, Dave, you will . . ." "I'm sure you understand, Florence, how any customer would be upset."

> You want your writing to be as effective as possible when you're conveying an idea, directing a course of action, or motivating someone to do something.

5. Use the Reader's Own Words

Use the recipient's own words when responding to something he or she has written. This is a surprisingly powerful writing technique. For example, let's say you are applying for a sales job with a cover letter and résumé. The job listing states "Sales Position. Independent self-starter sought for new sales position. Good verbal and people skills needed." Your cover letter might begin, "I am applying for your sales position. I am an independent self-starter with good verbal and people skills." Now, this has to be true, of course, and if it is not, do not write about what you are not. The point is, the more closely you can respond using the recipient's own language, the more effective your writing will be.

6. Get Feedback on Your Writing

When you are face to face with someone, you communicate in a variety of avenues that include words, tonality, and body language. Writing, for the most part, is one-dimensional. Before you write something important to someone, make sure it is right and that it communicates what you hope to get across. Set it aside for a while and come back to it later and read it to make sure it does communicate your message. Have a friend or co-worker read it for you and see if he or she gets the message.

7. Check Your Grammar and Spelling

Always spell check and proofread your writing for spelling and grammatical errors. Have your friend double check it for you. Simple errors of spelling and grammar will create a negative impression that will taint your message.

8. Credit Your Sources

If you are using someone else's words, be certain to give credit to the source. There is no faster way to destroy your message and its credibility than to use someone else's words as your own. My cousin, who has a doctorate, was grading a graduate thesis. As he read the student's submission, the words sounded familiar to him. The student had taken portions of my cousin's own thesis that he had written some time before and added them into his own thesis, as if they were his original writings without crediting the source. Needless to say, that student did not get credit for his thesis.

WRITE TO DISPEL EMOTIONS THAT INHIBIT YOUR PRODUCTIVITY

Writing may also help you better manage your emotions. If you have an issue with someone that you cannot get off your mind and this focus is interfering with your productivity, write that person a letter. Sit down with a pen and pad and write everything that is on your mind. Be specific. Use frank and harsh language. Compare that person and his or her behavior to despicable acts if you choose. Vent your spleen. Say it the way you want to say it. Do not worry about political correctness. Let that person have it with both barrels. Tell him or her what he or she did and how it hurt you.

When your letter is done, put it in a drawer and let it sit there for a few days. Then retrieve your letter and reread it. Make sure it says what you really want to say. If you wish, add more statements and condemnations, explaining how this person has made you feel and the trouble he or she has caused you. Get an envelope, address it to this terrible person, and put your letter inside. Seal the envelope, but do not put postage on it. Then put the letter back in the drawer. Go to bed this night with a feeling of relief, that you were able to get some of these bad feelings off your shoulders and onto paper. When you wake the next morning, retrieve the envelope containing your letter, tear it up, and throw the pieces into the trash. You don't have to send it. The act of writing alone will go a long way for you to get your feelings, which have been standing in the way of your personal productivity, behind you.

I recommended this technique to a student of mine. He went home that night and wrote nine angry letters. He had a lot of hurt in his life from a number of people. He slept better that night than he had in months and the next morning, he trashed all that he had written. The problems, the hurt, and the roadblocks to his personal productivity went into the trash as well.

———◆———

Here it is, in writing: Your personal productivity is in proportion to your ability to competently and confidently express your thoughts and ideas in writing.

18

BLAH RATHER THAN
BLAH, BLAH, BLAH

THE ART OF BEING CONCISE

———◆———

Many people take forever to say very little. You
know who they are. These are the same people
who spend a lot of time in meetings. They are the
ones who send e-mails that are as long as *War and Peace*.
They may have little to say, but they use many words to say it.
They can be boring. They waste time. They reduce productivity, their own and yours. More important, the longer the
communication, the less likely it will be read and acted on.

We all have that friend out there who likes to circulate the
latest joke via e-mail. The jokes are typically not all that
funny, but he or she sends them out anyway to a master list
of twenty people, including you. Then some of the twenty
recipients think they have a better joke to send out to the list
and soon your inbox is loaded with a bunch of e-mails from
the same people circulating their jokes that you do not care
to read. You then label all e-mail from these recipients as

trash. When these same people have something important to communicate, you may ignore that message. Likewise, the motormouth at the office may be ignored or avoided when time is short. In a world in which time seems scarce, people lose their patience with those who aren't concise when they should be.

The last thing I want to suggest is that all of our communications ought to be reduced to one or two words. There should be time in the day for idle chat. It leads to relationship building and a better quality of life. However, it is sometimes more productive to simply say "blah" rather than "blah, blah, blah."

As a practical matter, it is becoming more and more important to be concise as we drown in this era of information overload. We get more information in one day than our great-grandparents got in a lifetime. Think about it. On an average day one hundred years ago, you may have looked at a seed catalog and read a newspaper and a few chapters of a

> **It is becoming more and more important to be concise as we drown in this era of information overload.**

book, if you owned one. Today, we have information coming at us from all directions, including phone calls, voice mail, mail, faxes, and e-mails.

BE CONCISE WHEN YOU COMMUNICATE

Do you want to be more concise in your communications? The following are two short and simple suggestions.

1. Think Before You Speak (or Write)

Before you make that call, write that memo or e-mail, or plan a meeting, think about what you hope to accomplish. A lot of extended, unnecessary communication is in search of a purpose. When you know what you are trying to accomplish and when and how you need to achieve it, your communication will be more productive. Always think first about your intentions and your goals. This applies to work as well as personal life.

2. Say the Same Thing in Fewer Words

When you write an e-mail to someone, look it over before you send it. See if you can say what you need to say in fewer words. I bet you always can.

I teach a communications class. In it, I ask my MBA students to write a five-page paper taking a stand on an issue of their choice. The purpose of the five-pager is to persuade the reader to their point of view. They submit it, I grade it, and return it to them. I then ask that they rewrite the paper in four pages, but cover all the essential points from the five-page paper and still be effective persuading the reader to their point of view. They will eventually rewrite the same paper as a three-, two-, and one-page paper. Each rewrite must contain all that was covered in the original five-page work and still persuade the reader to their point of view. It's a tough assignment, but with practice, they get better at saying more with fewer words.

You can, too. Write something, then rewrite it several times, each time making it shorter than the previous attempt. The more you practice, the better you'll get.

———◆———

The bottom line is that concision requires you to be conscientious about your words. Use them sparingly for greater effect. Quality over quantity. Enough said?

19

SPEAKING TO AN AUDIENCE

◄———••———►

As I've mentioned many times now, productivity has a lot to do with your ability to communicate with others. Effective people know how to persuade and inspire others not only one on one but also in large groups. Most of us, however, freeze up when we need to address a crowd. Some studies suggest that the fear of public speaking is second only to the death of a loved one.

Public speaking is a learned skill. It is not innate or intuitive. I know this from experience. I have made my living speaking and communicating to groups around the globe and have made more than 2,000 presentations during the last twenty years. The truth is, I am a very shy person. It's true. My performances always get high marks from my audiences, but what I do and how I do it is a skill I developed with practice.

As a kid, I was sometimes terrified of meeting people. It was almost impossible for me to ever introduce myself to a stranger. Around seventh grade, I had to write a report on what I wanted to be when I grew up, and, for some reason, I said I wanted to be a public speaker. I did not really know what a public speaker was or that it even existed as a profession. I did not see myself specifically conducting time management and personal productivity seminars as I do today. But I did see myself standing before groups communicating in some fashion, maybe as an entertainer.

I knew, even at that early age, that if I wanted to be or achieve anything, I had to do it, not just talk about it. So, at every opportunity, I put myself in a position to speak by raising my hand first in class and even speaking out of turn.

My first real public speaking presentation came in seventh grade when I ran for treasurer of the student council. I did not really care if I won the election. I ran because I would be able to make a five-minute presentation before the entire school at an assembly.

As the day approached, I prepared my five-minute speech. I practiced, practiced, and practiced some more until I had it down cold. I added a little humor as well. My mother taught me about the importance of humor as a communication device. Humor always makes a message easier to deliver. I knew many of the speeches that day would be dry, so a little humor in my speech might give me an edge.

The big day finally arrived and I was a basket case. The

school assembled and the speeches began. They did them in order. As I anticipated, there were many boring speeches. First the presidential candidates, then the vice presidents, secretaries, and finally the treasurer candidates. It was done alphabetically as well, and being a W, I was the last of about a dozen speakers.

As I approached the podium and looked to the audience of 50,000 people (oh, all right, it was only 500 but it sure seemed like 50,000!), I was so frightened that I could not make out the faces in the crowd. I shivered as my speech began. I was on automatic pilot. The words, so well rehearsed, flowed in nervous ripples. I was so anxious that I could not even hear myself.

Then I got to my funny line. When the line hit, the audience responded. Several elbowed their neighbors as if to say, "Hey, wake up! This guy is funny!" They gave me a standing ovation. (Nevertheless, I lost the election.)

When I walked off that stage, I took some valuable lessons with me. First, I did not die. This shy kid could survive the big presentation and live to tell about it, so, maybe, just maybe, there really is nothing to fear about making a public speech. Second, I learned that I could be good at public speaking.

HOW TO EXCEL AT PUBLIC SPEAKING

Good communicators sell their ideas. They move people along and are better leaders. They are more productive in their own lives, speaking to others and getting the reactions they seek.

Now that I've given thousands of public speeches, I can say with some confidence that the ability to address large crowds is a skill that you can develop over time. The following are the best ways to get started.

1. Just Get Out There and Do It

Speak whenever possible. Put your hand up first. Ask questions of the speaker at the end of a lecture. Go to the podium at the Boy Scout parents' dinner, the town hall meeting, the business conference. Sit in the front row. Volunteer to give a class at your local community center, library, or religious organization. Practice, practice, practice speaking in public all the time. This is the best way you can improve your public speaking skills.

> **Good communicators sell their ideas. They are more productive in their own lives, speaking to others and getting the reactions they seek.**

2. Sign Up for a Class

If you are in need of significant, rapid improvement in this skill area, sign up for a public speaking class. You can find them offered through adult education programs and at local colleges. Private companies offer this training as well. Join Toastmasters International (www.toastmasters.org), which is a wonderful organization open to everyone who wants to improve their presentation skills. There are chapters in all major cities worldwide.

THE PREPARATION THAT MAKES PERFECT

Now let's assume you've actually agreed to make an oral presentation next week to a group of fifty people you have never met. It may be to the sales department at work or at your daughter's PTA meeting. Here are a few tips to build your confidence and make that oral presentation a hit.

1. Keep the End in Mind

What are you trying to accomplish with your presentation? What are you trying to sell? Is it a pitch for more money for an advertising budget or to get the PTA to back a fund-raising idea? Focus on what you have to say to get what you want. Prepare a clear and concise presentation that gets your point across within the time you have been allocated, or if no time has been specified, then in the least amount of time.

2. Prepare an Outline of Your Speech Beforehand

You can write your presentation out, word for word, but I don't recommend it because it will come across as too scripted or canned. It's better to prepare your speech in an outline form, listing the major points you will cover. The outline format will be more natural. Your introduction should explain what you will speak about. The bulk of your time will be on the meat of your presentation, the reasons and rationale of what you are speaking about. Finish with a brief summary of what you covered.

3. KISS—Keep It Simple, Speaker

Do not speak over your audience and lose them with your impressive vocabulary. Do not speak down to them. Speak to them at their level.

> **Prepare your speech in an outline form, listing the major points you will cover.**

4. Get to Know Your Audience in Advance

Before I do a presentation, I get as much information as I can about my group. Age range, men versus women, education, job responsibilities, other seminars they may have attended, and anything else that might be helpful to know. The more I know, the more comfortable and confident I am. Then I arrive early and meet and greet with a handshake as many people as I can before my presentation. For a keynote speech where there may be hundreds, it is difficult to meet everyone, but I will shake hands with as many people as I can, looking them in the eye and thanking them for coming. I do this for my audience. They get to meet their speaker first. It makes my presentation more personal. But I also do it for me, so that when I stand before them, I am looking at familiar faces.

It is critical to establish a rapport with your audience as soon as possible. This tends to make them more receptive to your message. I make it a point to try to look everyone in the eye several times during the first few minutes of my talk. Your goal is to connect with each person. Time and again, even with large audiences of hundreds, people will come to me after my talk and say, "It was like you were talking directly to me." Yeah, I was.

5. Be Aware of Your Tone and Rhythm

Should you speak quickly or slowly? Fast is better and more engaging, but not so fast that you are tripping over your own words. Soft or loud? I prefer soft, as people have to pay closer attention to follow what you are saying. If it is a motivational speech where my task is to fire up the audience, I will prefer to vary the tone and rhythm of my speech. I will go from soft to loud and back again throughout, but my emphasis generally will be on soft.

6. Pay Attention to the Setting

If possible, arrive early to check out the setting.

- *Is the lighting okay?* Is it too bright or too dark? Will the ceiling lights wash out my slide presentation? Hotels sometimes have wall sconces, decorative lights that are annoying to look at if they are behind the speaker. I turn them off.

> **It is critical to establish a rapport with your audience as soon as possible.**

- *Is the temperature okay?* If it's too warm, your audience will fall asleep. I try to get the thermostat set to 68 degrees, not cold enough to hang meat, but cool enough to keep them awake.

- *Is your equipment okay?* I check out the sound system, the overhead projector, and my laptop and LCD projector, if I'm using them. Are they all working? Do you have spare bulbs, batteries, and other backup equipment?

- *Is the number of seats appropriate for the turnout?* Empty seats look bad. Lots of empty seats look terrible. I was in Chicago at a hotel ready to present to a group of thirty people. When I arrived at the function room, the hotel had set up 300 seats. I quickly got the setup people back to take away the extra 270 chairs. If I didn't, I would have been speaking to thirty people scattered throughout the room. In fact, I will typically ask that we set up a few less chairs than the number I am expecting. For example, if I am planning on thirty people, I will set twenty-seven chairs. Most of the time, one or more will not be able to attend and if everyone shows up, I personally make a big fuss, getting an extra chair just for them. It creates a "standing room only" atmosphere.

- *Is the seating arranged correctly?* For small groups of thirty or less, I like to have them seated in a horseshoe shape where they get to see each other. It makes for an intimate environment. For longer sessions, like a full-day seminar when note taking will be important, I have them seated at tables, classroom style. I stand in the front and rehearse to this empty room, all to make sure it is set up and working the right way and to give me a familiarity with the room so that when I stand to speak, I try to go to a place where I've been before. It's a stress reducer. And I do this before the audience arrives. One final note: It is not professional to be moving tables and chairs around when your audience begins to arrive.

7. Make a Good First Impression

First impressions are lasting and you do not have a second chance at a first impression. When speaking to a group, you typically have but a few minutes to make that great first impression, to get past the threshold of whether or not they are going to listen to you in the f7irst place, never mind do what you are going to ask them to do. If you start off on the wrong foot and fail to capture your audience, you may have lost them.

THE "DON'TS" OF PUBLIC SPEAKING

The following are five things you should *never* do when you're a public speaker.

1. Don't Try to Fool Your Audience

It probably won't work. Audiences are very perceptive. They know when the speaker "walks the talk." They also know when the presenter is just giving a book report, having spent a little time in preparation to learn about the high points of the topic presented. When you are the keynote speaker, your audience ought to sense that you are not just a gallon of water, but rather a fountain of knowledge.

2. Don't Read Word for Word from Your Text

Your audience wants to experience what is in your heart and mind. Notes to guide you through the important points are fine, but if you are reading from a text, you may as well hire a professional actor who is trained to bring a script to life. Know your material cold. Tailor it as you deliver it. As your audience reacts to a particular point, expand on it. Feed them what they hunger for.

3. Don't Use Inside Stories

Don't mention some event or anecdote about someone whom most of your audience will know nothing about. It will alienate most of your audience and keep them in the dark. It will make them feel that they are not among the chosen few.

4. Don't Make Your Audience the Butt of a Joke

Humor is a wonderful communication tool (if you are funny). Self-deprecating humor that reveals your own vulnerabilities and foibles works. Stories about people and events, other than your audience, if done in good taste, will set the tone for a positive learning environment. But if you direct the barbs of your humor directly to your audience, you set up an "us versus him or her" climate that will interfere with your message getting out. Attacking an audience, even if not meant to offend, will tend to make them defensive and distrustful of you.

5. Don't Go Over Your Time Limit

You have a contract with your audience. Their obligation is to be attentive. Yours is to deliver the material that was promised and to do it within the announced time frame. If you are given twenty minutes, finish in twenty minutes.

8. Be Yourself

Don't try to be another speaker. The best speakers are the natural ones, the ones who are themselves, warts, annoying gestures, and all. It does not mean you are the world's leading expert on your topic. You walk the talk. You speak from the heart.

9. Use Visuals and Other Nonverbal Aids

People learn through three different inputs: visually, what they see; auditorily, what they hear; and kinesthetically, what they feel through their emotions. We use all three modalities, but we are predominantly one rather than the other two. About a third of your audience will be the visuals, a third will be the auditories, and the remaining third the kinesthetics.

The point is, if you stand at a podium for an hour delivering your speech, about a third will be with you, the auditory folks, and the other two-thirds, the visuals and kinesthetics, will probably have lost their attention. Build in all three communication paths in your presentations. Make a good auditory presentation. Speak clearly so that people can hear you. Modulate your voice from time to time. And bring in the overheads, the slides, and the handouts to help make your points. Gesture as you make points. Move from the podium from time to time. You are appealing to your visual folks. Then add some emotion. Every topic lends itself to an opportunity for humor or deep empathy. Build it in your speech. You will be a hit.

———◆◆———

Who knows? You may even begin to enjoy public speaking. Remember: By spreading your message to many people at one time, you're exponentially increasing your productivity.

20

MEETINGS WITH MEANING

How to Get the Most
Out of Every Meeting

———◆———

When asked about the biggest productivity killers at work, Americans always talk with exasperation about meetings. Many of my clients gripe about how they spend most of their working days in meetings and only have time for their "real jobs" after hours. In the spirit of shorter meetings, our time together in this chapter will be efficient, useful—and as concise as possible.

BEFORE YOU MEET

Meetings are the biggest institutional time wasters. Whether you are a meeting organizer or just a participant, bear the following in mind to maximize your meeting time.

1. Is the Meeting Really Necessary?

If you are going to be a good time manager, you have to get away from giving your time to those who simply demand it and, instead, give it to those who deserve it. Now, I do not mean that in any negative or arrogant way. It is just that the demands for your time far outstrip your supply. The next time you are asked to join or organize a meeting, think about whether ot not the meeting is really necessary.

We are all creatures of habit. We always go to the weekly staff meeting because we have always gone. Nobody ever asks a question like, "What if we had it every other week rather than weekly?" I can't assure you that everyone will go along with you, but change happens only when we consciously take a step back and examine what we are doing rather than continuing to do what we do out of habit.

How can you tell in advance if a meeting is necessary? Ask what's on the agenda. "Sure, I would like to meet with you, but, so that I may be prepared, what are we going to discuss? This way I can be prepared for our meeting." In many cases, it is some relatively simple matter that can be handled between two or three people in a few minutes rather than taking ten people an hour to meet face to face.

If the meeting isn't necessary, say so. One of the most powerful words in your time management vocabulary is *no*. *No* does not always have to sound like *no*. You can say, "This is not a priority for me right now," "I have too much on my plate already to really do a good job for you," or "I won't be able to meet until later in the week."

Use the words with which you are comfortable. The point is if you are ever in a position where you cannot say "no," then you are saying "yes." If you don't stand for something, you'll fall for everything.

2. Are You Necessary to the Meeting?

If the meeting is necessary, the next question is "Am I necessary?" Now, I do not mean that in some deep philosophical sense, but rather, do you get anything from this meeting? Do you contribute anything to it? If the answer to both questions is "no," see if you can avoid the meeting. Or perhaps, the first half hour applies to you but the remaining hour and a half does not. Ask if you can be excused after that first half hour.

Everything will not work 100 percent of the time, but if it works 50 percent of the time, you will be that much further ahead. Some things in life we can change, and we will. Some things in life we can't change and we're going to have to live with them. Try it. Ask. The worst you will be told is no.

3. Have an Agenda

Have you ever been in a meeting and put on the spot to discuss a subject that you are not prepared to discuss?

The next suggestion is to have a written agenda. Just as you have an agenda for your day (your to-do list), have a written agenda for your meeting. It does not take a lot of time to prepare. Circulate it among the meeting attendees before the meeting so that you can secure feedback and allow everyone the opportunity to be prepared (or ask the meeting's coordinator to do so). Maybe the feedback will allow you to remove items from the agenda, saving everyone time. Maybe items can be added to make the meeting more productive. If no one else is willing to do this, volunteer to do it and everyone will benefit.

Include a starting time in the agenda and stick to it. Has this ever happened to you: It is 2:00 P.M., the scheduled start of the meeting, and only four of the twenty invitees are present. What do you do? You wait, and the others drift in and

> **One of the most powerful words in time management is *no*.**

the meeting finally begins at 2:25. When that occurs, the people who were on time are punished.

The ending time is equally important. If you come to my meeting and I tell you it will end at 4:30 P.M., you can take that to the bank. Now if it runs over for five minutes, please do not hang me. But the point is, if I tell you 4:30, I will not keep you there until 5:45. I presume you have plans and commitments and if our business requires more time, we will schedule a subsequent meeting, but I will get you out of this meeting as scheduled.

4. Assign a Time for Each Agenda Item

There is a rule that applies here called Parkinson's Law. It states, in part, "a project tends to expand with the time allocated for it." If you give yourself two hours to talk about one agenda item, it will take two hours. Without reasonable guidelines, any single item can dominate the entire meeting. Has this ever happened to you: There are ten items on the agenda and the meeting is to last two hours, but the first item takes an hour and forty-five minutes. We can (and do) discuss to death any issue.

Assign time for each item on the agenda. Set a time frame. For example: "2:00–2:20 New Benefits Package: Bernice; 2:20–2:45 Change in security procedures: Gene." This will tighten up the discussion.

I was once at a PTA meeting at my son's elementary school. Three hundred parents were in the gym for a two-hour meeting. There were ten items on the agenda to discuss but no time frames set for each item. The first item on the list was: "Should the PTA spend $75 for the teacher supply fund?" Global warming, peace in the Middle East, and the state of the economy, these are some of the issues that capture my attention, but $75 for the teacher supply fund?

A motion was made and seconded and now the issue was open for discussion. The first person stood up and spoke in favor of the motion. "It's a small request. The teachers are good to our kids. Let's spend the money." Sounded reasonable to me. The next person stood and spoke against the motion. "No, we shouldn't spend our money this way. Our funds should be used for assemblies and special events. I will vote 'no.'" Another interesting point. I was not sure now how to cast my important vote. I felt as though I needed more information.

Without reasonable guidelines, any single item can dominate the entire meeting.

←——•——→

Well, I was in luck because seven other people lined up behind the microphone (microphones are dangerous things to put into public meetings), each of whom wanted to put in his or her two cents' worth on this great issue. The debate raged on for an hour and a half; 450 man-hours spent to decide on how to spend $75—and we had nine other agenda items to go! Halfway through the debate, the fellow next to me said, "Come on, you and me, let's kick in $37.50 apiece and get the hell out of here!"

The bottom line: Assign time for each item or you'll waste time.

DURING THE MEETING

In spite of all these preparatory tools, there are some people out there who will be tough to rein in, so here are a couple more ideas that will be useful the next time you're asked to participate in (or help lead) a meeting.

1. Be on Time (and Enforce Timeliness Among the Other Participants)

There are some people out there who absolutely believe that they cannot make meetings on time. Ever run into them? Here is what happens: A meeting is scheduled for 2:00 P.M. At 1:58 this person gets up from her desk to go to the meeting some thirty paces down the hallway and her phone rings. What does she do? She picks it up claiming that it could be an important call. At 2:06 she walks out of the office and runs into one of her staff members who asks, "Can I see you for a minute?" What does she do? She stops to talk. Eventually, she drifts into the meeting at 2:26, convinced that she could not have done otherwise.

Now here is the irony. This same person is *never* late for a 2:00 P.M. flight. She lets the phone ring, she'll tell the staff member she doesn't have any time, and she'll rush to get to the airport on time. How come? She cannot take the risk of getting bogged down in something that will keep her from connecting with that ride to the airport.

If you have to meet with someone who does not respect agreed-on beginning times, schedule that meeting for a Friday afternoon. For example, if you know your discussion should take only an hour and you know that person wants to leave the office at 5:00 P.M., see if you can schedule your meeting for 4:00. This way the meeting will end on time

> **If you have to meet with someone who does not respect agreed-on beginning times, schedule that meeting for a Friday afternoon.**

because you have backed it up against that person's commitment to leave work on time. Or schedule it one hour before any other commitment that you know this person has.

2. Resort to Extreme Measures

A final suggestion is to have no chairs. That's right. No chairs. Everyone will file in and say, "What's going on? Where are the chairs?" Your reply, "Oh, this won't take too long." People will have to stand for it! Literally. The point is this: The more comfortable you make a meeting, the longer it will last, and if that is your objective, then roll in the heavy leather chairs, turn the lights down low, and provide a variety of refreshments (always offer brewed regular and decaf coffee). Your meeting will last a long time. I am not in favor of making things uncomfortable for people, but the simple truth is that the more comfortable the meeting, the longer it will last; the less comfortable the meeting, the shorter it will last.

On the topic of furniture, those plastic-molded seats common in fast-food restaurants are designed to be just a little bit smaller than the average butt. Whereas a typical seat is set at an angle so you can comfortably slide into it, these seats are often set dead level. Why do fast-food restaurants do this? Because they do not want you to sit there all day with a cup of coffee. They want to turn the seats over quickly so they will require fewer seats. The average person gets uncomfortable sitting in these seats after ten or fifteen minutes.

You can use this to your advantage. If you have to meet with someone this weekend, your insurance salesperson, for example, and you need to get the information but you do not want to spend a lot of time with him or her, suggest a meeting at a fast-food restaurant. On the other hand, if you would like the meeting to last some time to develop a relationship, perhaps with a prospective employer or a new customer, choose a nice cushy restaurant. Just by the choice of the venue you can affect the time and the quality of your meeting.

<hr/>

One last thought on the topic of meetings. I'm not sure how practical this idea is, but it did help a client of mine to cut back on company meetings to a fraction of what they were before. They instituted a policy that required that you apply, in writing, for permission to hold a meeting before you could schedule it. Now that's a creative solution!

> **Just by the choice of the venue you can affect the time and the quality of your meeting.**

21

SIX DEGREES SMARTER

MAXIMIZING YOUR CONNECTIONS

❖—◆—❖

If you had to make a list of all your contacts, how many people would you name? If you're like most people, you probably think that you have, at most, a couple hundred connections. Not so. There's a pretty good chance that you have more than 1,000 contacts. How? Look at it this way: A contact is someone you know well enough that when you call, he or she will take your call.

Test yourself. Did you graduate from high school? Did you go to college? How many people did you graduate with? Two hundred? Three hundred? How about the people you met on the job or through the many jobs you may have had? You have neighbors? Do you know the bank teller? Do you have a dentist? A family doctor? Put them down. How about relatives? Relatives? Sure. If they'll take your phone call. (I know. Some won't! Leave them off your list.)

Get the picture? You start to think about all your contacts

and list them and the numbers grow to an average of more than 1,000 contacts.

Now, you might think, "But I haven't seen or spoken to these people in years." But if you can call them today and if they will accept your phone call, they *are* contacts.

My most valuable asset is my network of contacts. There is not a business or personal problem I cannot solve with help from my contact base. Knowing others helps us to learn from others. The people you know can give you introductions that would take an inordinate amount of time otherwise. Contacts save you precious resources of time and money. (For tips on how to meet new people, see Chapter 22.)

DISCOVERING YOUR CONTACTS

"Out of sight and out of mind." It always amazes me how difficult it is for us to retain all these details in our heads. Putting this information into writing is a far more effective way to preserve your contact base and prevent information from slipping through the cracks.

I started to make a list of my contacts back in my college days. I would write up a three-by-five-inch index card for every new person I met. Today, I have all that data on my computer. I now have more than 5,000 contacts in my database and can cross-reference any number of ways to find the right contact I need to reach. I have categories for relatives, neighbors, clients, doctors, dentists, suppliers, and church friends.

Of course, you will not be able to keep current information on everyone. You may not be able to track down old childhood or college friends ever again. Or maybe you can. With the Internet, it is fairly easy to locate someone if necessary. (One site, www.classmates.com, contains contact information for hundreds of thousands of people, organized by the names of their high schools and colleges and the years of graduation.) To keep your contacts current, it's a good idea to contact everyone on your list once a year. E-mail is an easy way to do this. Some people send out holiday cards to stay in touch. In the end, your list will always be fluid, changing, evolving, and growing.

I keep my contacts in a computer database. This way I can easily categorize my contacts by profession and interests, such as tennis players, political enthusiasts, and pet lovers. Many people appear in many different categories. The value here is that I can search by several criteria to find just the right person. For example, with a few strokes of the keyboard I can locate all the plant managers in my database who enjoy tennis and have been a client and are situated in a particular state or city.

Here is a good example of how this is useful. I received a call from a potential new client in Houston, Texas. She asked if I ever get to Texas to conduct my seminars. "In-deed, I do," I told her. "I have presented in all fifty states at one time or another."

"Have you ever been to Houston?" she asked.

"Yes, many times."

"Good," she continued. "Send me a few references from the Houston area. I will contact them and maybe we can do some business."

I hung up the phone and I honestly could not think of one person that I knew in Houston. I knew I knew people there, but I could not, for the life of me, get that information to surface in my brain. It's almost like being at a party and a friend says to me out of the blue, "Tell us a joke! Come on. You're funny. Tell us a joke now!" You might be funny and you might have an inventory of funny jokes in your head, but being blindsided like that may block you.

So, I went to my contact database and typed in a search for "Houston, Texas" and up came nine contacts. After I

Contacts save you precious resources of time and money.

←——•◆•——→

called to verify their information, I found three who were perfect references that I sent along to my new potential client. If I had to rely on my memory only, I probably would not have recalled any.

If you have an average of 1,000 contacts and each of your contacts has an average of 1,000 contacts, you are closely connected to 1,000 people and only one more step removed from 1 million people and two steps removed from 1 billion people. Let's say you are in a job search and you would like to speak directly to vice presidents of manufacturing for medium-sized manufacturing companies in your area. What is the chance that there are one or more in your own contact base to contact? Better yet, what are the chances that there are probably several in your contacts' databases? The chances are high, and if you let your contact base know that you need to contact that type of person, no doubt many would respond with a name and telephone number allowing you to call these plant managers and introduce yourself and your job campaign with "Our mutual friend, Sandy Smith, suggested I give you a call."

Perhaps you are involved in a charitable fund-raiser. How many in your contact base could contribute to your cause? Tons, and remember, they will take your call and people are almost always willing to help an acquaintance, if they are asked.

MAXIMIZE YOUR CONTACTS

The following are six steps to maximize your contacts.

1. Make Your Database

Every time you meet someone new, get as much contact information as you can and add it to your list of contacts. There is power in writing things down rather than trying to remember everyone you know. Whom do you include in your database? Everyone. Everyone you know, everyone you have met. "Contact" means you have had "contact." Leave no one out. Include name, address, and contacting information. Start with your family, then your neighbors and co-workers. How about the co-workers from your last job(s)? How about your high school and college graduating classes and the teachers you had? Do you belong to a pro-

> If you have an average of 1,000 contacts and each of your contacts has an average of 1,000 contacts, you are closely connected to 1,000 people and only one more step removed from 1 million people.

fessional association, a club, or a church? The bank teller, your dentist, your bookie—they all go on the list.

2. Categorize the List

This is when a software program is really useful. Identify those who are friends, acquaintances, customers, suppliers, politicians, and professionals, and those who enjoy golf or tennis. The more categories you can place people in, the quicker you can access the right contacts. Many of the software applications also allow you to do a keyword search, which is especially useful when you can remember only the first or last name of someone, or the name of the company where, he or she works. Through my database, there is not a problem I cannot get answered for myself and those whom I want to help.

3. Feed the List

Once you create the list, you have to continue to feed it. Update, correct, and add more and more people as you meet them. Many of us meet dozens of new people every week. I spend about an hour every week feeding my list. It's a chore. It's not convenient, but it's worth it.

4. Join an Online Networking Web Site

One easy way to link up and keep track of the friends of friends of friends is to join popular networking Web sites such as Friendster, Spoke, Ryze, LinkedIn, Tribe.net, and ZeroDegrees. Another popular site of this kind is the afore-mentioned Classmates.com. Networking sites create data-bases of friends, family, and business contacts, and many are searchable by name, interest, place, and type of connection.

5. To Have a Friend, Be a Friend

Being someone else's connection is how you can make all this data work for you. Networking is not one-sided. If you want this tool to work, you have to be like a good politician. You must do things for people. You help them first. I'm al-ways clipping articles I come across and sending them to people I know. "Thought you might be interested in this." I send many birthday cards. I call many of the people in my database at least once a year to see how they are doing and what they may need that I can provide for them. Then when it comes around "election time," when I need something, I feel no hesitation to ask for a return favor.

> **One easy way to link up and keep track of the friends of friends of friends is to join popular net-working Web sites.**

BE A CONTACT, TOO

Now, it is not enough to add people to your list as you meet them and then call them only when you need help. If you want to have a friend, you must be a friend first.

Look to our politicians as role models for effective networking. Take Edward "Ted" Kennedy. Kennedy has served for the last forty-four years as the Democratic senator from Massachusetts. One might argue with his politics and the stands he takes on various issues, but no one can doubt that he is a superb networker. My grandmother Nana could vouch for that personally.

Nana lived out her life in Massachusetts and was a diehard Red Sox baseball fan and a lifelong supporter of the Republican Party. She rarely missed a Red Sox game during the season and had always voted Republican. As a diehard Republican, Nana was not a fan of the Kennedys.

Nana's son, Dick, my uncle, passed away unexpectedly in the mid-1960s after having retired from a career in the U.S. Navy. Because of his military service, he was afforded a burial plot in Arlington National Cemetery. In the years after his funeral, family members would visit Dick's grave and report back to Nana that it was not well kept. Nana felt unhappy about it, but, given her advanced age, she was powerless to do anything.

Family members suggested she write to Ted Kennedy for help. After much urging, she finally wrote him a letter describing the problem and asking for his help. She received a letter back from the senator promising to look into the matter and report back to her. About a month later, Nana received another letter from Senator Kennedy informing her that he visited the grave site and found that it was indeed in need of care. He requested the grounds people at the cemetery to regrade and reseed the grave. Kennedy also enclosed several before and after photographs to show the work that had been done. He closed his letter assuring my grandmother that his staff would visit the grave again in six months to ensure the new grass took hold. And they did.

Every election thereafter until her death, Nana voted for her favorite politician, Senator Ted Kennedy, and she asked her friends to do the same.

6. Use It

Whenever I start anything, a new marketing program, a career move, or buying a house or car, I think of my network first and talk to those in my database who may be able to give me some answers, can refer me to someone who has the answers I need, or can open the doors for me. I have saved tons of time and money and advanced my success in so many ways by tapping into my network database first.

←——•——→

There's a nonpartisan lesson in this: Service your network as often as possible. Make contact with as many people as often as you can, offering your help whenever possible. Be your own politician. The more contacts you help, the stronger your contacts are, and the more productive you'll be.

22

A BIG SMALL TALKER

MAKING NEW CONNECTIONS

◆————◆

O kay, you've created a database of your existing contacts—your high school and college friends, colleagues and former colleagues, babysitters, fellow pottery class students, and so on. But you're not done. In fact, you're never done with your contact database. It should always be growing, and you need to keep feeding it. How? By making more and more contacts all the time.

Many people dread meeting strangers and having to strike up a conversation with them. It can be awkward at best and painful at most as you struggle to get something off the ground. It may be especially hard if you don't already have a common context like a workplace or a shared friend. What do you do? You improve your skills. As I've said before, good communication skills open doors for you. People you meet can present business and networking opportunities and solutions to your problems in less time than it would have taken you without their help.

BUILDING RAPPORT

You create relationships by building rapport. You build rapport by finding things in common, searching for connections. Once commonality is established, warmth envelops this budding relationship and provides the opportunity for true friendship.

But it's hard to build rapport from scratch. That is why lapel pins, signature rings, and bumper stickers are popular. It's also why fraternities and sororities, bowling leagues, knitting circles, sports teams, and alumni clubs exist. They are ways to announce, nonverbally, an identity with which others can identify. Instant rapport.

Creating that initial rapport, the ice breaker if you will, is difficult when people are resistant, suspicious, and a tad untrusting. This is compounded if you ask the wrong type of questions, closed-ended questions that beg for a "yes" or "no" answer only, without real dialogue.

"Do you live in town?"

"No."

"Weather sure is nice, isn't it?"

"Yes."

"Great party, right?"

"Yes."

"Did you see the game last night?"

"No."

"Is that your car?"

"No."

"Do you like tennis?"

"No."

You probably feel like the dentist pulling teeth from an uncooperative patient.

Keep the following points in mind when you meet someone new, and a world will open up to you.

1. Ask Open-Ended Questions that Call for a Dialogue

Let's say you just started your career today with the newspaper, the *Daily Bugle*. You are the new cub reporter and the editor gives you your first assignment. There has been an accident at the intersection of Washington and Main Streets and it is your job to go out, gather the facts of what occurred, and write a story about what happened.

Like a good reporter, you go to the scene armed with six powerful, open-ended questions to help you get the information you need: who, what, where, when, how, and why? As you interview the witnesses at the scene, you ask the six questions in various forms.

"Who are you?"

"I am Joe Sparks and live in that house over there."

"What did you see?"

"I saw car A run a red light."

"Where did it occur?"

"Right here in the middle of the intersection of Washington and Main."

"When did it happen?"

"About twenty-five minutes ago."

"How did it happen?"

"It looked like driver A was reaching for something on his backseat and not paying attention to his driving. Car A ran into car B proceeding through the intersection with a green light in his favor."

"Why did it happen?"

"Driver A was totally intoxicated. After the collision, he got out of his car and could barely stand up, staggering about, slurring his words, with a heavy smell of alcohol about him."

When you meet someone new, use open-ended questions involving who, what, where, when, how, and why as if you were a cub reporter. These types of questions work because they give the other person an opportunity to talk about the most important topic in their lives, themselves.

The following are some examples of some open-ended questions.

- "Where do you live [or work]?"
- "How long have you lived [worked] there?"
- "Why did you get into that line of work?"

- "What are your favorite hobbies?"
- "Who do you know that is a good auto mechanic here in town?"
- "When did you decide to do that?"
- "How does this neighborhood keep its sidewalks so clean [or dirty]?"
- "Where do you like to go when you have to shop for clothes?"

An elderly woman was hosting a benefit event many years ago. She was known by many for her charitable works. She met a young man standing by the doorway and he asked, "Why are you here?"

She replied, "I am the one hosting this benefit party."

The young man, who was new to the community, did not know this and asked, "How did you get into hosting benefits as magnificent as this one?"

She went on for the better part of twenty minutes talking about how her late husband left her with much money, how

> **When you meet someone new, use open-ended questions involving who, what, where, when, how, and why as if you were a cub reporter.**

she felt obligated to share it with others in need, why she chose to set up a foundation for giving, where it was located, and how it was doing. The young man wished her a good day and excused himself. A friend of the philanthropist approached her and asked, "Who was that young man?"

The lady replied, "I don't know. I didn't get his name. But what a wonderful conversationalist he was!"

2. Observe How People Present Themselves

A good opportunity to craft your open-ended questions is to observe the pictures, diplomas, trinkets, class rings, T-shirts, and things that people display, bring, or wear. Why? Because they are intentionally exhibited to make a statement to the world about who they are. If you are visiting a person in his or her office, home, or other personal space, note the personal things he or she has on display. Is there a tennis racquet on a bookshelf? Maybe there is an awards plaque on display for some volunteering work he or she did. Pictures are great. They show family, friends, and interests. Maybe he or she had diplomas on the wall.

Observe and ask. "You're a tennis player. I have never played, but how do you get an interest in the sport?"

"What an adorable picture of your children! [They better be adorable!] Tell me who is who and what they are doing now." With this question, some will be able to respond for hours!

3. Find Commonalities

You may get another person to like you by following numbers 1 and 2, but true rapport is established only when you connect the things he or she is saying about him- or herself to yourself and your own experience. This way, the other person identifies with you. Keep asking the open-ended questions and keep him or her talking. The more he or she talks, the more information you receive about potential points of commonality and mutual benefit. You will then find yourself naturally responding with your own "me too" statements. "You enjoy tennis? So do I! A year or two ago I was playing and it was so hot . . ." The rapport builds from there.

←———•◆•———→

The best part about productivity is that you can start today. Put this book down, strike up a conversation with a stranger, and see how far you get.

> **True rapport is established only when you connect the things he or she is saying about him- or herself to yourself and your own experience.**
>
> ←———•◆•———→

23

ME, INC.

GETTING FEEDBACK AT WORK

————◆————

O n one level, productivity is about managing your-self, your workload, and your own expectations. On another level, it involves managing other people, whether you're delegating to them or working with them. On yet another level, productivity means being able to manage those above you. For many people, the person on the career ladder above them is their boss. The way you communicate with your boss helps determine how and when you meet "big picture" goals involving career and life.

Now, how do you manage up?

First, take a step back and imagine that you are the pres-ident of, say, a bank. What possible reasons would cus-tomers be favoring your bank over the competition? Perhaps your branches are conveniently located. Maybe you offer a higher rate of interest on certificates of deposit or your mortgage interest rates are lower than anyone else's in town. In fact, there may be dozens of reasons why your customers patronize your bank.

Would it be wise for you to assume which reasons are important to your customers? Probably not, because you might be wrong. So, you probably would want to poll your customers from time to time to determine why they chose to do business with your bank.

A good question to ask your customers would be "How are we doing a good job for you, and in what ways do we need to improve?"

The answers you receive will probably be all over the place. Maybe customers think you are doing a good job for them when you provide products and services at the lowest price, that you are conveniently located, that you have a friendly staff, or combinations of these reasons and others. As president of the bank, you want to know if the number-one reason they came to your bank is safety and security and the number-two reason is the convenience of your branches and so on. This way, your advertising programs could highlight these hot buttons and you could drive more customers to your bank. They might give you suggestions

> **The way you communicate with your boss helps determine how and when you meet "big picture" goals involving career and life.**

for ways the bank could improve, such as Saturday hours or more ATMs. By polling your customers, your bank would be more effective and efficient at giving customers what they want and targeting new customers. Simple.

Now to my point: Each of us *is* the president and sole stockholder of a major corporation, Me, Inc. And, in the context of this discussion, think of your boss as a customer whom you want to satisfy. Your boss has a lot of control over your future raises and promotions. Why not ask, "How am I doing a good job for you, and in what ways do I need to improve?"

You may assume your boss thinks you are doing a good job because you are innovative and creative, coming up with new ideas. In reality, however, he or she may be threatened by that and feel more comfortable when you do not rock the boat. (In that case, you might want to take your "business" elsewhere.) You may assume that your boss is comfortable with your performance when there are no complaints (no news is good news). But he or she may measure your performance on the number of unsolicited compliments he or she receives from others about how well you are doing your job. The point is, you need to find out and direct your attention to these hot buttons. If you need to improve your performance, you'll know what to do and how to do it. Make sure to listen well and ask specific questions that will help you make the most of the conversation.

Some people feel uncomfortable about asking their boss to evaluate their performance. The problem is, it is a question that will have to be addressed sooner or later. For many, it is addressed too late, usually at an annual review when you discover that you did not get the raise or promotion you thought you were entitled to. Only too late would you realize you had been going down a path contrary to your boss's desires. The effect may be that your raise or promotion is delayed or lost, not because you were not working hard enough but because of a misunderstanding of what your boss really wanted from you. Miscommunciation is one of the biggest causes of lost productivity.

———◆◆———

The bottom line is that you need to be proactive, and polling your boss is key to your career productivity. It is a good idea to ask him or her to evaluate your performance several times throughout the year because expectations can change.

> **Miscommunication is one of the biggest causes of lost productivity.**
>
> ———◆◆———

24

MIND CONTROL

MANAGING YOUR EMOTIONS

———◆◆————

Imagine that you are doing a great job planning your daily to-do list or you just made a great new connection who might help you in your career. You're ready to conquer the world. Then someone comes along and says one negative thing to you and your whole day goes in the bucket. Or you receive a couple of pieces of bad information at the beginning of the day and your productivity goes south as you reel from the upset.

Let's face it: We are heavily influenced by what others say to us, what we say to ourselves, and what is said to us from the media. When something bad is communicated to us, we are inclined to respond strongly. A whole day can be blown by one piece of upsetting news. If you are not in a positive emotional state, all the planning tools in the world will not help your productivity.

When you are in a balanced and positive emotional state,

people tend to cooperate with you. Things go your way, which, of course, makes you more productive. In fact, personal productivity has a lot to do with the cooperation of other people, and this goes far beyond delegation. You'll have better networking opportunities and business contacts. You'll have more encouraging pats on the back.

Given that emotional balance, the cooperation of others, and productivity go hand in hand, this chapter focuses on how to put your best face forward.

THE FACE YOU SHOW THE WORLD

Here's a fun exercise to do with a small group. Ask each person to think about someone in his or her life whom he or she truly admires and respects. Then ask him or her to list a half dozen qualities about this wonderful person, one-word adjectives that come to mind. Write down fifteen to twenty of the characteristics your group has identified.

> **If you are not in a positive emotional state, all the planning tools in the world will not help your productivity.**

Some common responses include thoughtful, caring, helpful, humorous, loving, steady, honest, strong, knowledgeable, appreciative, friendly, articulate, open, sharing, and devoted.

Some of the characteristics you will list will be learned qualities, something the person had to acquire such as the ability to speak several languages or know geography. Others will be more of an attitudinal quality, a way the person lives and relates to others such as being caring, loving, open, and thoughtful. Every quality can be enhanced through learning and attitude, but each one is predominately more one than the other. Go down your list and identify which items are more learned and which ones are more of an attitude.

What you'll discover is that most of the list will be made up of attitudinal qualities. We tend to admire people more for their attitude than for what they know. The truth is that how you're perceived by other people is as important to your success and productivity as how much you know.

Now pretend that we have before us Mr. and Ms. Negative, who are nattering nabobs of negativity. They have all the statistics memorized about why things will not work. Mr. and Ms. Negativity are afraid to do something new because of a fear of failure. They recite a litany of complaints whenever you talk to them. Have you run into a Mr. or Ms. Negative in your life? We all have.

That person is wasting his or her life. Worse, he or she is repelling others because negative people are stressful and draining. Moreover, a Mr. or Ms. Negative has set him- or herself up to attract other negative people who want to share his or her stories of dread, and these stories create a shared reality of fear and discouragement. Finally, of course, a negative person tends to be unproductive. Even when fear is a motivation, it often backfires.

IT'S HOW YOU REACT TO IT

Where do these negative, limiting emotions come from? Try this. Ask someone the customary attitude check question, "How are you?" or "How are you doing?" You will typically receive answers that tend to be either positive or negative.

"I'm really great." "I'm just fine." "I'm okay." Or "I'm lousy." "Not so good today." "I'm really bummed out."

Then ask the follow-up, kicker question, "Why do you feel so up?" or "Why do you feel so down?" and most of the

> **Whenever negative information comes your way that could result in diminishing your productivity, respond in your own mind with two words, "That's great!"**

time you will hear an answer that points to an external event (or series of events) that has created the emotional state he or she is in.

"I got a raise, that's why I'm so up." "I just had a good customer." "It's Friday and the weekend is here." Or "My boss really brought me down." "My wife hurt my feelings." "I got a flat tire, that's why I am upset."

Can a boss bring you down? Can your spouse hurt your feelings? Can a flat tire make you upset? No, they cannot. What causes the upset is how you react to it.

You cannot have an emotion, positive or negative, without first having a thought. We have positive and negative thoughts. Positive thoughts produce positive emotions and negative thoughts product negative emotions. And whatever emotional state we find ourselves in, we take action consistent with these emotional states.

So if your friend, a salesperson, says that her customer upset her, she is only half right. Certainly the feeling she feels is real. Her statement of emotion is accurate. But the event with the customer did not cause the emotion. Your friend's processing of the event caused the emotion.

Let's break it down. Your friend encountered a customer who said some unkind things to her. Now, if she did not hear the remarks in the first place, she would not have had any emotional reaction. But she did hear those nasty remarks and she is feeling down because she placed negative thoughts around those negative comments from the customer. It may have gone like this, "He shouldn't have said those things to me." "This is unfair." "Why is it the customers always pick on me?"

Of course she's upset, but the customer did not create the upset. She did by her reaction to what occurred.

Now let's say you do not want to feel negative emotions when people are rude to you, when you get a flat tire, you're delayed in traffic, or some other minor disappointment happens. Will you experience these disappointments in daily life? You can count on them—with regularity. And while you cannot always control what goes on outside, you can control what goes on inside of yourself and how you react to it.

Here's my advice: Whenever negative information comes your way that could result in diminishing your productivity, respond in your own mind with two words, "That's great!"

> **You're being unproductive for as long as you dwell on an incident and generate negative emotions about it.**

When you say "That's great!" it places a positive thought up front in your mind and it leads you to answer the question: Why is this seeming disappointment so great?

A customer hassles you and you say to yourself, "That's great . . . because he could have said a lot worse than that! Because he could have said that to someone else not as strong as me and caused a lot of unnecessary harm. Because, in spite of the harsh tone, this is a good way for me to learn about our customer service."

You learn you have a flat tire and you say to yourself, "That's great . . . because I drove off the exit ramp pretty fast earlier. If the tire had let go then, this car might have tumbled over. Because it happened here in the parking lot where it is safe and well lit. Because I have a spare tire. I'd really be in a mess if I didn't have the spare. Because the other three tires held up! Imagine if all four tires went down!"

You are delayed in traffic and you declare, "That's great . . . because I can use this time to get caught up on my daily planning. Because we were all rushing out here on the highway and heading for an accident. Because I can reschedule my appointment and use this time to make some phone calls."

I am not suggesting to you that you paper it over when bad things happen to you. This is not some namby-pamby response to real pain. What I have shared with you is the only sensible, healthy, practical, sane, and productive way to respond to most of life's little upsets.

When we receive a disappointment, and we will with regularity, there is only one thing we can do about it. Fix it. Does any of your upset change the fact that you have a flat tire or you had a tiff with a colleague? No. Are there things you can do in the future to prevent bad things from happening again? Yes. But you're being unproductive for as long as you dwell on the incident and generate negative emotions about it. You'll feel lousy and your outward physiology will reflect the unhappiness that is going on inside. It's difficult to get people to cooperate with you when you're negative. And for as long as you're dwelling on your bad day, you won't be productive. Guaranteed.

It is only when you can convince yourself to see the flip side of upsetting news—the "that's great!"—that you will be able to be productive even in your darkest days. Like speed reading, better writing, diary-making, and all the other exercises in this book, changing your response to bad news will take time and effort. In fact, there's a good chance that it will be even more difficult than anything else you read here. But seeing the good in the bad is the only way to change your emotional state from disappointment to possibility.

In this section you'll start thinking about how the tips and techniques learned in the previous chapters apply to your life goals—the measure of your productivity over a lifetime. Those life goals must be established for all areas of your life— health, family, financial, intellectual, social, professional, and spiritual. Each are complements to the others and they must all be in balance. To live a genuinely productive life, you need to understand this, the "big picture."

PART 4　THE BIG PICTURE

25

YOUR CORE VALUES

Going Back to Basics

Think about all the things you do each day—going to work and doing what is required, dropping your kids off at music lessons, running to the gym, going shopping, watching TV, and so on. As you read this, stop for a moment and make a mental list of everything you've done in the last couple of days.

Now ask yourself if your actions are consistent with your values.

Your values are the truths and foundation blocks on which you build your life. They are the principles that you feel strongly about that create a compass in your life. The point of values is that as long as your actions are consistent with them, you will set yourself up with a solid foundation for permanent success. But whenever your actions are inconsistent with your values, you invite failure. If your actions defy your values, everything that has meaning to you, all your productivity is bound to go to waste in the long run.

Some of my values include spending quality time with family, honesty, good health, humor, and loyalty. You may agree with some of these or perhaps you do not. Values are very personal things.

To illustrate how important they are, let's take quality time with family as an example. Most people have that as a value. Let's say you have a job that requires sixty hours a week. In addition, you attend classes three nights a week because you're working to earn another degree. You're also the treasurer of the bowling league. And all these responsibilities translate into no time for family. The insidious thing about it is that the people around you might praise you for your achievements. But you won't be fulfilled because family is one of your values and you don't have time for them. You'll feel an emptiness.

That emptiness may grow and soon you may abandon your undertakings and, in effect, sabotage your own productivity. But if you could instead identify the problem, that

> **If your actions defy your values, everything that has meaning to you, all your productivity is bound to go to waste in the long run.**
>
> ←—◆—→

it is out of balance with your basic values, then you can make the adjustments to carve out the time to spend with family. There is always enough time for the important things.

Let me share some interesting statistics with you:

- *One out of eight people does not want to go to work on Monday morning*
- *One out of five people moves every year*
- *One out of three people changes jobs each year*
- *One out of two marriages winds up in divorce*

If your values are imbalanced, you might do unreasonable things to try to correct the problem. You might look outside of yourself and your situation, thinking that any change is good. You might say something like "What can I change? I know. I'll move. Surely if I get into a new community I will feel better." And so you move. Now, every time you move, does that take away from your personal productivity? Sure thing. How many days did you have to work just to pay those three guys with a truck to move you? How many weeks (or years) will it take to make new connections and establish roots?

You might look to your job, thinking that is the cause of the problem. Does changing your job help you spend any more time with your family? Nope. And every time you change a job, does that take away from your personal productivity? Yup. You lose seniority and have to go through a new learning curve. Certainly to change a job for good career enhancement makes sense, but doing it for the wrong reasons does not solve your problem and is counterproductive.

Maybe you think the actual problem is your significant other. You haven't been seeing much of him or her, and perhaps you blame him or her. Leaving certainly won't solve your problem. It will enhance it.

But if in this case you could determine that the problem is a mismatch between your values and your actions, that the solution rests within you, you could make the adjustments to bring your actions more in line with these values. We can always make whatever we are doing—where we live,

> **By knowing your basic values, and using the list to examine your actions, you can make changes in your life to maintain your productivity while staying on the same path.**

where we work, and the relationships we are in—work for us and feel good about it inside when we have a good handle on what our basic values are in the first place. But without a clear vision of these values, without a compass, your actions can easily become counterproductive.

Take the time now to actually write down the list of the things you value most in your life (family, honesty, career success, humor, travel, etc.):

Don's Basic Values:

Quality time with family
Honesty
Good health
Humor
Loyalty

Where do you find your values? Most of them are already in your head. Be conscious of them. One of the best places I have found values is during inspirational reading, a time I set aside each morning to absorb uplifting material to start my day on a positive note. As you read inspirational materials, the concepts you identify with will pop out at you. That is how I discovered humor as one of my basic values. I was reading about Will Rogers, the humorist, and as I learned about his life it hit me. Humor. That's an important part of my life. I added that to my list of values.

There is a practical benefit of writing your values down. For me, it helped when one day something didn't seem right. I was going about my daily activities, my speaking schedule was filled, there was money in the bank, and it all should have felt good. But for some reason it just wasn't right. I took a step back and went through my list of basic values and there it was—humor. My seminar material to me had become rote. The humor for me (but hopefully not for my audiences) was no longer there. Could I fix that? In a New York minute. I could easily add new material and it was bright and fresh again for me and helped me to move forward in this business.

Without an articulated and clear list of values, I would not have been able to recognize what was wrong. By knowing your basic values, and using the list to examine your actions, you can make changes in your life to maintain your productivity while staying on the same path. No big, time-wasting changes are needed to find that internal satisfaction.

◆━▶

Take a moment to examine *everything* you are doing. Are you getting to where you want to go in your life?

26

ACHIEVING YOUR GOALS

GETTING TO THE FINISH LINE

B y this point in the book, you should have the tools and knowledge to start applying your productivity skills toward a goal. There's a good chance that you picked up this book with a goal in mind (apart from simply being more productive). Now, with your daily planning techniques, your enhanced ability to retrieve and absorb information, and your new and improved communication skills, you should be able to get started.

But read on first. Did you know that most people who try to attain their personal goals fail? This is especially true of behavior-changing goals such as weight loss, smoking cessation, alcohol and drug abuse programs, and, yes, even productivity. In fact, the sad truth for dieters is that most of them who actually do achieve their weight loss goal will be at or more than their previous weight level one year later. There are similar failure rates for other programs designed to alter behavior.

When I discovered this, I was intrigued and wanted to find out why.

As I looked further, what was puzzling me was that most behavior modification programs are technically correct. For example, if you follow what most weight control programs suggest, you will lose weight. The addiction control program methods are likewise sound. So why do these goal-setting programs fail so broadly? Certainly, it is not due to lack of desire on the part of those who try these programs to achieve their personal goals.

I believe I have found at least part of the answer.

WHY RESOLUTIONS FAIL

If I am involved in weight control, I say that I want to *lose* weight. If smoking is a problem, I will want to *quit* smoking.

> Did you know that most people who try to attain their personal goals fail? This is especially true of behavior-changing goals such as weight loss, smoking cessation, alcohol and drug abuse programs, and, yes, even productivity.

I may want to *stop* drinking. I may want to *discipline* myself better. What are lose, quit, stop, and discipline? All negative-sounding goals. And that's the problem.

Subconsciously, we move toward positive goals and away from negative ones. We are pleasure-seeking organisms who seek pleasure and avoid pain. Lose, quit, and stop are all negative goals. (The first three letters of the word *diet* are *die*.)

So why do we get involved in these negative goal programs in the first place? Typically, we are motivated by negative emotions such as fear or anger. We fear what is happening to our health or are angry with ourselves for what we have done or not done, and, based on that emotion, we submit ourselves to do these negative things such as lose, quit, and stop, much like we would punish a child.

Then one of two things occurs. We fail and nothing more really matters. Or we succeed. As we succeed, we start to get confident and somewhat cocky. "I haven't had a cigarette in three days!" "I finished everything I set out to do this week!" As we gain confidence, the negative emotions that brought us into the negative control program in the first place start to weaken. And when these negative emotions disappear, we go right back to our previous behavior.

WHAT TO DO

The following are some ways to put yourself in the right mind-set and discipline yourself so that you'll have more momentum when confronted by negative emotions. Some of these tips will sound familiar, as I've addressed them in other chapters in the context of procrastination.

1. Motivate Yourself with Reward, Not Punishment

To increase your chances for achieving any goal, you need to frame it as a positive goal with a positive outcome. Don't tell yourself you are going to lose weight. Say, "I am going to get into a size 8 dress by next summer." Instead of quitting smoking, how about, "I am going to get fresh, pink new lungs and more money in my pocket." Rather than stop drinking, instead see yourself waking up with a clear head, without a frequent hangover. Rather than disciplining yourself, you are taking control of your time to achieve your goals.

We move more naturally and comfortably toward the achievement of a positive goal. The mind will more readily

> **We move more naturally and comfortably toward the achievement of a positive goal.**

accept a positive goal and not automatically try to find ways and rationalizations to sabotage us as with a negative goal.

2. Put Your Goals into Writing

List anything and everything you could possibly want in your life. Do it as a child makes up a Christmas wish list. When kids make their wish lists, they don't worry whether or not Santa Claus had a recession during the year. They feel he will deliver everything.

How many goals should you have? The answer is enough. I have about fifteen different goals that I work on, not every day, but over the long stretch. When I share this with others, it sometimes stresses them out. Perhaps you're a person who feels more comfortable working on just one or two important goals at a time. No problem, work within your level of comfort.

All goals do not have to be major accomplishments. Put down the small ones, too. Put both big and small goals into writing. Left unwritten, they tend to elude us as they drift off into a "someday" pile.

Separate your goals by category using the seven vital areas: health, family, financial, intellectual, social, professional, and spiritual. Under health, maybe a weight loss goal, cosmetic surgery, or a new commitment to exercise. Under family, spending more quality time with your spouse or significant other or a fantastic family vacation. Under financial, how about getting an additional $50,000 in the bank or $100,000 or more? Under intellectual, what about reading 100 books over the next year or learning a new language? For social, perhaps doing more entertaining at home or joining a bowling league? Under professional, perhaps securing a new professional designation or a change in your career altogether? And under spiritual, what about signing up to teach Sunday school or learning meditation? Hey, why not? Every dream is possible.

Don't get all hung up on which category to place a goal. It will serve only as a placeholder.

3. State Your Goal in Terms of Quantity and Deadline

I talk to many people about their goals. "Tell me your most important goal," I ask.

"I want to be rich. That's my goal," they say.

"Rich? Rich like Midas?" I ask. "Rich Little, the comedian?"

"Okay. My goal is to have more money," they explain.

"Well, that's easy to achieve. Here's a dollar. That's more money."

"Oh, I get it now. Well, my goal is get $20,000 more in the bank."

"Now we're talking! Now I understand. 'Rich' and 'more

money' are too vague, but $20,000, that's clear. Now, the only thing missing is 'when.' Why? Because, if we don't have deadlines, we procrastinate."

"My goal, then, is to get an additional $20,000 in the bank two years from today."

Now he or she has a goal that's quantified and with a deadline. Now they are able to break that goal down into its little itty-bitty component parts. If the goal is to acquire $20,000 in two years, that's $10,000 a year. And a year consists of twelve months. That's about $800 a month. And a month consists of four weeks. That's $200 a week. And a week consists of five business days. That's about $40 a day. (I've rounded the numbers and not factored in interest for the sake of simplicity.)

I don't know about you, but the notion of getting $40 today toward my goal is a whole lot more manageable than the idea of getting $20,000. You just don't find that kind of cash lying around the streets do you? I'm intimidated by $20,000. But $40, that's a single step, the first step on a journey of a thousand miles.

I see many possibilities for achieving the $40 daily goal. I could sell that old lamp in my living room. I could give up bowling this Tuesday night. I could work some overtime or maybe cancel the cable television. And while it may be a struggle, it is doable. And if I can do it today, I can figure out a way to do it again tomorrow, then the next day, the next, and the next again. And if I continue for two years, I will have reached my goal.

4. Visualize Yourself as Having Already Achieved the Goal

Goal achievement begins with a strong internal reason for having it. A goal to please others often does not have the strength to carry you through the hard work and sacrifice needed to accomplish it. You must have a clear picture in your mind of having already achieved your goal.

For example, you cannot achieve the goal of owning your own business until you see yourself as an entrepreneur first. Visualize yourself already having what you desire. The body will follow the mind. Do it first thing in the morning as soon as you wake up. Remind yourself several times throughout the day that you are becoming a business owner. As you drift off to sleep, see yourself in your new home office. Imagine. You can never do too much of this and until you do enough, you cannot begin to do what will be necessary to

> **Visualize yourself already having what you desire.**
>
> ⟵ ◆ ⟶

achieve the goal. But once you have done enough, when the picture is firmly implanted in your mind's eye, then your actions will follow that picture. Life does become a self-fulfilling prophecy.

5. Find People to Support You

Once you've established the picture of yourself as a business owner, you need to get the "how to" to achieve your goal. Be careful with whom you share your goals. There are two types of people you will come across: enablers and disablers. An enabler is someone who has already achieved your goal or at least believes in the process. A disabler is someone who has never achieved your goal and does not believe in the process. (In addiction recovery programs, the term *enabler* has a negative connotation. Here, in goal planning, it has a positive meaning.)

Team up with one or two enablers, people whose judgment and optimism you trust, and brainstorm the possibilities. Forming this coaching group will help you to scale heights you may be unable to scale on your own.

There are many more disablers out there than enablers, more people who will try to discourage you from going after what you want in your heart than people who will encourage you forward. In fact, the people closest to you will turn out to be the biggest disablers in your life, not because they don't love you, but because they do love you. It's just that they don't believe in the process and they see you proceeding down a path to harm.

Recall some of the things you may have heard from some well-meaning loved ones over the years. "You lose twenty-five pounds?" "How many times have you tried that and failed in the past?" " I like you just the way you are." "You go into your own business? You've never done that before." "You're buying new furniture? You know your father and I did not have new furniture until we were well into our forties! Where are your priorities?"

6. Get the Right Information

Let's say that you would like to acquire a new Mercedes, a fine luxury car. Here's how I would get the know-how to achieve that goal. I would identify someone who already has accomplished my goal, someone who already has the car I desire. This could be a stranger, maybe someone in the parking lot at the mall. I would approach this person and

> **Team up with one or two enablers, people whose judgment and optimism you trust, and brainstorm the possibilities.**
>
> ←——◆◆——→

say two things: "Nice car" and "How do you get a car like this?"

I would not be so abrupt as to confront a stranger and simply blurt out "Nice car! How'd you do it?" We would have a little small talk first, but these would be the two important points I would make.

I have practiced this technique of complimenting people hundreds of times and have never had a failure. I may not always get the same amount of information with each request, but I always succeed with the technique. Compliment a person and he or she will be much more likely to help you. Why?

The three most powerful words in the English language are "I love you." Do I suggest that you approach a total stranger in a parking lot and say, "I love you"? (Hey, maybe you'll get a ride!) Of course not. But when you say "I love you," you don't always have to use these words. What are you doing? You are paying value to that person and there are few who are suffering from complimentary overload. So, as you approach that stranger who already has the car you want and you remark, "Nice car," you are saying, "I love you." You are paying value to that person.

There is another reason this technique works 100 percent of the time. What is the number-one topic of conversation everyone has in their lives? Themselves. People love to talk about themselves above all other topics. When people talk about themselves, do they like to talk about their failures or successes? Why, their successes, of course.

GOALS TAKE TIME

I take a shiny penny out into the woods where there are 2,000 rocks, place it under one of the rocks, and tell you, "There's a penny out there under one of those rocks. Why not go get it?"

Now, let the penny represent your dream, your goal, and I am telling you that the "how to" to your dream is out there, just go and get it.

Under the worst-case scenario, how many rocks might you have to look under to find the penny, the path to accomplishing your dream? All 2,000. You might find the penny under the 10th rock or the 300th rock, but if you are willing to look under all 2,000 rocks, you will find the penny. The penny is out there independent of your search for it.

> **Compliment a person and he or she will be much more likely to help you.**
>
> ←—◆◆—→

THE BOAT GOAL

Let me share an example of how powerful goal-making can be. Some years ago my wife, Nancy, and I were into boating. The best we could afford was an old wooden, leaky boat. It wasn't much, but we enjoyed it. We had a dream, though. We wanted a bigger boat, a more modern boat, perhaps a fiberglass boat with less maintenance. Maybe a trawler-style pleasure boat, forty-three feet in length with a fly bridge, twin diesel engines, three staterooms, and a galley. Yes, we dreamed big.

You should have heard what many of our friends said when we announced we were going to find a way to acquire such a boat. My best friend at the time remarked, "You're going to do what? You're going to try to buy a big new boat like that? Why, you've never tried to do that before!" he admonished. Because I've never done it in the past, I could not possibly do it in the future.

Listening to our disabling friends did a number on Nancy and me. As they threw up the obstacles to which we did not have answers, we began a journey of self-doubt that led us toward abandoning our dream of that nice new pleasure boat. But finally I took my own advice and Nancy and I went to a nearby marina, found the boat we wanted tied up there, knocked on the door, and greeted the owner.

"Nice boat!" I said.

When I said, "Nice boat," it was an "I love you." I was complimenting him on his achievement. Do you think he was proud of his boat? Of course. When I asked, "How do you get a boat like this?" I was asking him to talk about himself and his success. And that he did.

He invited us aboard for the courtesy tour. He showed us everything and gave us information we didn't know existed. For example, we thought we would have to pay for a boat over a three- or four-year period, like a car loan, making the payments prohibitively high. "No," he assured us, "you can finance this type of purchase over a fifteen-year period so the payments are reduced and more affordable, like a home mortgage." Armed with this information, we then met with the boat manufacturer and got more answers.

Almost eighteen months to the day from when we decided to acquire a boat, we took delivery of a brand-new forty-three-foot trawler.

This is powerful stuff, if you use it.

○

But here is how many people approach achieving their goals. They will say, "Yes, I would like a promotion (or whatever goal they have in mind), and they will walk into the woods and start searching under the rocks for the how to. They will look under 300 or 400 rocks, and, not finding the penny, will return to the office and say, "There, I told you. There's no penny out there for me. Poor me. My life is going nowhere."

Is the penny, your goal and dream, out there for you? It sure is, if you are willing to search for it. There has never been a problem that did not carry with it a corresponding solution. Nature is not so cruel as to give us insoluble problems. A solution is always out there, if you look for it. Keep going until you find the penny and, most of all, enjoy the process.

27

THE PRODUCTIVITY PYRAMID

Piling the Blocks

———◆———

In 1994, the Winter Olympics took place in Lilleham-
mer, Norway. I am a skier, so I was particularly interested in the downhill event when Tommy Moe, from
the United States, won the gold medal in downhill skiing.
What do you think the skill differences were between Moe
and his competitor who came in last place? Very little. For
the last-place finisher, it was an edge of a ski that caught or
a moment's inattention that caused him to lose time and
finish last.

How did Moe get the gold medal? Do you think he woke
up late and opened the shades, "Hey what's going on out
here? A ski race? [Yawn] Medals? Gold, silver, and bronze?
[Stretch] I dunno. Maybe I'll try it, see if I can rent some
skis. Boy, this hangover is miserable!"

Did Moe do that? Of course not! He planned, condi-
tioned, practiced, and made sacrifices during the years
leading up to the day of the event. And without all of that,

his productivity that day would not have secured him a gold medal and a place in history.

What makes any of us think we can have a gold medal if we do not do what the champions do?

UP AND DOWN THE PYRAMID

Let's review everything we've discussed about productivity in the previous chapters. (As I've said before, repetition is the key to effectively remembering an idea.)

By this point in the book, you should have the building blocks of a productivity pyramid that looks like the drawing on the next page.

From bottom to top, the pyramid features the following levels.

1. Adequate Sleep

Adequate sleep is crucial for a productive life. Studies show that about 75 percent of the U.S. population is tired almost any time of the day, mostly due to stress and overwork. So many people experience highly stressful days and are always reacting to stuff thrown at them. Then, when bedtime arrives, many will not get quality sleep. Without a good night's rest, much of what we have discussed cannot work well for you. You can place all sorts of good time manage-

PRODUCTION

DAILY PLANNING

SEVEN VITAL AREAS

BASIC VALUES

WAKEUP HOUR

ADEQUATE SLEEP

ment tools into your toolbox but if you are just too darned tired to open it, they do you no good.

2. The Wakeup Hour

Up another level is the one-hour wakeup. As discussed in Chapter 3, take advantage of your alpha state. In alpha, your brain waves and physical cycles are slowed and it is then that you are at the highest level of learning receptivity. Take advantage of this by getting up an hour before your normal waking time and do positive visualization. Read inspirational material and take a walk. What you do in this first hour of your day will set the pace for the remainder of your waking hours.

3. Basic Values

The next step is the notion of basic values. Values are the foundation blocks on which we build our lives. Mine include honesty, loyalty, and humor. No amount of success can ever be permanent and lasting unless we act consistently with them. Everyone has values, but few of us ever articulate them or write them down. (See Chapter 25 for a discussion about creating a values list.)

Use your list to identify problems that inhibit your productivity or happiness. Use it to remind yourself of what matters in your life and make adjustments accordingly.

4. Seven Vital Areas

Building on your basic values is the concept of seven vital areas: health, family, financial, intellectual, social, professional, and spiritual—and the necessity for balance among them. Life has these seven dimensions to it, and like a seven-legged table, if any one leg, never mind two or three, is longer than the rest, it can upset the entire table. While you may value your social life different from the way I value mine and while you may value your intellectual life different from the way I value mine, we all have a social life, an intellectual life, and five other dimensions. You may not spend equal amounts of time in each area or time every day in each area, but, in the long run, if you neglect any one area, never mind two or three, your table will collapse.

5. Daily Planning

Next comes planning on a daily basis for today, tomorrow, and the rest of your life. Planning helps you establish your life goals: becoming a CEO, parent, novelist, painter, and so on. Surprisingly, very few people know what they really want to achieve in their lives. Goal planning starts with being able to describe how you want your life story to end.

Goal planning informs the to-do list that you prepare

> You can place all sorts of good time management tools into your toolbox but if you are just too darned tired to open it, they do you no good.

each night as part of your daily planning, taking time each night to plan out the next twenty-four hours. As a result of working on your to-do list in daily planning, you will have developed a road map for your tomorrow, having built in all the things you have to do, but, more important, having built in all the things you want to do. You will have also prioritized your items and then subprioritized within each so that all of your scheduled tasks are laid out in a way that gives you the biggest bang for the buck for the next day.

6. Production

Finally, at the top, is production. This is the actual *doing*. All the talking, writing, and planning you do will not substitute for the doing. This is the area where you will spend the bulk of your time, but look how small it is in relation to the overall system. It is all the steps beneath it that make the production so meaningful and important.

WHERE DO YOU STAND?

As you take a glimpse out into the real world, where do most people fit in on the pyramid? At the top, production, let's say, for the sake of argument, that virtually everyone, nearly 100 percent of the people out there, are doing the job, getting paid, and paying their bills. They are staying out of trouble and living day by day. Nothing wrong with this. I offer no criticism.

How many people are at the next level under it, preparing a daily to-do list? Our studies show that about 70 percent of business people use a to-do list most of the time. But the standard to-do list is not adequate. If I ask these same people, "Tell me a little about your family goals," they'll say, "Family goals? What do family goals have to do with time management?" What do basic values have to do with productivity? I have found that just one in twenty are able to identify his or her life goals. Most people give good lip service to the concept of lifelong planning, but few actually follow through. The to-do list you create in daily planning should encompass goals beyond mere routine tasks. Include steps related to family, health, spirituality, and so on. As you know now, productivity is more than just making up a good list to administer the have tos of life. It should include taking time to do the want tos, and you get there by integrating them with your entire life in balance.

Now to the seven vital areas. Over the years, I have run into only a few people who have disagreed with the philosophy of keeping your health, family, financial, intellectual, social, professional, and spiritual life in balance. These people will tell me that they do not have the time just now in their lives to create this balance. Their situation is such that they can focus only on one or two areas for now, perhaps just the financial and professional areas. They have recently taken on new responsibilities at work or are caught up in a job search that leaves them no time to devote to the other areas of their lives. But just as soon as they get over their current hump, they will have time to create this balance in their lives.

I think they have it all backward. I do not believe that this notion of balance is some reward that comes to us once we become successful. I think it is a necessary ingredient to become successful because if we are out of balance we create stress in our lives that interferes with long-term, permanent success. You can do a great job at work but if you ignore your health and it fails, you risk losing all that short-term gain through sickness and illness. Ignore family and you might wind up in divorce court.

So many people fall into the trap of becoming what I call uni- or duo-dimensional. (Don't try to look these words up in the dictionary. I just made them up.) They build their lives on one or perhaps two legs all the while taking inadequate time for the other areas, telling themselves this is a temporary situation and "as soon as I get over the hump" then I will have time for these other areas. First, it takes at least three legs to balance a table, right? And life can be cruel.

The point is, if you are living your life built on seven legs of the table and if life should take one or two away, you have five or six other legs to hold you up. But what if you are supporting your life on only one or two legs and life takes one or both of these from you? What happens to your table? It collapses. This notion of balance is not a reward once we become successful. It is a necessary ingredient to get there.

Moving down the pyramid, how many people identify and live by their personal set of basic values? Very few. And while we all have them, few people take the time to think about them and write them down. Remember, no amount of success in your life will be permanent and lasting unless it is consistent with your unique set of basic values.

How about that one-hour wakeup routine? How many people practice this? Not many. So many people wake up at the last possible moment (or a little later) and slam, bang have this chaotic fire drill just to get out of the house in the morning. They use the first hour or so at work to wake up and get up to speed. Have you ever noticed that when you

> **Most people give good lip service to the concept of goal planning, but few actually follow through.**

lose an hour in the morning you spend the rest of the day looking for it? It sets you behind the whole day.

How about adequate sleep? As discussed, three out of four people, at any time of the day, will complain that they are flat-out tired. If you are not rested, it is tough to muster the energy to do the right things to have a productive day.

———◆———

It's never too late to begin a genuinely balanced and productive life. Now that you know what it takes, do it. Get a good night's sleep and prepare for your morning wakeup hour. Do it now. Review your values. Find your balance. Start your daily planning.

Resources

The following pages contain additional resources related to productivity, including logs. Logs work as periodic diagnostic tools because they afford you the opportunity to see problems in their entirety so that you can take corrective action. They're meant to help you see the "big picture" of how you spend your time. Use these tools to enhance the tips and techniques you've learned throughout the book.

THE TIME LOG

You have gone on vacation, had a great time, and spent a lot of money. To make that investment last and enhance its value, many of us will take a lot of pictures and maybe even put them in a nice photo album. The photo album gives us the big picture, the overview of our fine time away.

How about if we apply this same concept for your day? Imagine a series of snapshots of specific moments in a normal day of your life. If you could get a clear picture of how your time was being spent, you would then be in a position to take corrective actions and adjustments so that you could enjoy greater productivity.

You cannot use a camera for these snapshots. Instead, use a time log. The time log does the same as the camera,

TIME LOG

GENERAL CATEGORIES

Date: _____

(Start Time)

Time of last entry	N I M		N I M		N I M		N I M		N I M		N I M		N I M		N I M		Total Hours
Total time for day																	

TIME LOG

8:25 (Start Time)

Date: __Monday, April 4, 2005__

GENERAL CATEGORIES

Time of last entry	Meetings	M I N	Telephone	M I N	Selling	M I N	Interrupt/Daydream	M I N	Mail	M I N	Research	M I N	Reading	M I N	Personal/Family	M I N	Misc.	M I N
9:00																	Planning 35	
9:12							Bill 12											
10:00	Staff Mtg. 48																	
10:10																		
11:15			Return Calls 65															
12:15					Smith 60													
1:15							Bill 20							Lunch 60				
1:35																		
2:45												Jones 70						
3:15					Jones 30													
4:00													Book 45					
4:50	Sales Manager 50																	
5:10							Bill 20											
5:30														Travel 70				
6:00													News. 30					
6:30														Dinner 30				
7:00														News 30				
7:30																Planning 30	
9:00													Sat. Review 90				
11:00														TV 120				
Total time for day	98		65		90		52		10		70		165		260		65	
% of day	11%		7%		10%		6%		1%		8%		19%		30%		8%	

Total Hours	515 min. 8.2 hrs.
	100%

permitting you to take a series of snapshots throughout your day, developing a collage or photo album so that on review, you can take steps to enhance your overall success.

This sample time log was set up for a salesperson to monitor and improve her day. You can make adjustments to your own time log to fit your particular situation. Photocopy the blank log for your own use.

In the sample log, the salesperson's day is broken down into the nine most common ways she spends her day. They include meetings, telephone activities, selling, interruptions, daydreaming, working with the mail, conducting research, reading, time for personal/family, and, finally, a miscellaneous category for the items that do not fit elsewhere.

Some of these column headings might be appropriate for your day. If not, just change them to fit the nine major ways your time is actually spent. Periodically, throughout the day, stop to take a "snapshot" of how your time is spent by filling in how long you spent in each column. Take into account how productive the time spent was by labeling each item A, B, C, or D.

It's inconvenient to have to deal with the time log during your day, but taking the time to enter the information does produce a wealth of data.

Can you wait until the end of the day to fill this out? No. Did you ever notice that when you try to estimate how long something is going to take, it almost always takes twice as long to actually accomplish it? The same thing occurs for most of us when we look in hindsight to figure out how long something actually took. So, if you wait until the end of the day to reconstruct the day, the information will typically be inaccurate. It takes but a few seconds to log in the time spent after each major period occurs. Take the time to do it as you go through your day.

Run the time log for a period of three to five days. If you run it only for a day or two, you might get a distorted picture of how your time is actually unfolding. Three to five days will tend to even out these distortions and give you a more accurate picture.

Having run the time log for several days, the saleswoman has accumulated a wealth of information. First, she adds up each column to determine the actual amount of time being spent in each area. She has spent ninety-eight minutes in meetings, sixty-five minutes on the telephone, ninety minutes selling, and so forth. Next, she calculates the relative percentage of each column as it relates to the entire day. In the lower right-hand corner, she totals up the entire day. On this day, she tracked 875 minutes or 14.6 hours. Divide each column's total number of minutes by the total number of minutes tracked for the day, or 875.

In the first column, she spent ninety-eight minutes in

meetings. If she divides 98 by the total of 875, the result is approximately 11 percent of her day was spent in meetings. The "11 percent" is inserted at the bottom of the meetings column in the "percent of work day" row. Next, she spent 7 percent of her time on the telephone, 10 percent selling, and so forth.

Whatever it is you do so well to produce great results in your day, the time log will show you exactly how much of your time is being spent on the things you do so well.

PUTTING YOUR TIME LOG INTO PRACTICE

After you have run your time log for a period of three to five days, take a plain sheet of paper and label it with four columns:

A | B | C | D

Next, go back through the time log and take the actual amount of time recorded in the small minute blocks and put it under the appropriate column depending on how productive that time was spent. Just using the first three entries in our sample time log for planning, "interruption with Bill," and the "staff meeting," the sheet would look like this:

A | B | C | D
35   48   12

Continue posting the rest of the entries from all the time logs run for three to five days and then add up all the A time, B time, C time, and D time.

If you are going to have a good and productive period, do you think it is a fair expectation that 100 percent of your time will appear under the A column? Of course not. Are you going to have some D time in your day? Certainly. You are going to look for D time during your day! We all do. D time serves a purpose. You are not a machine or a robot.

What if you discover that the larger segment of your time was spent in the A and B columns and the smaller segment of your time was spent in the C and D columns? Would you feel that you had a good and productive day or week? I should think so. Did you have some wasted time? Yes. But so long as the bulk of your time was under the A and B columns, I think you can feel you have had a productive period.

Percentagewise, how much of your time should be spent under the A and B side as opposed to the C and D side? How about 80 percent A and B and 20 percent C and D? How about 50 percent A and B and 50 percent C and D? How about 20 percent A and B and 80 percent C and D? Do you know what? *You* get to select the numbers. That is the exciting thing about personal productivity. You get to define it. I have no right to tell you that you are not a productive person unless you achieve a certain level of ratios that I have preset. You are the only one to determine how productive your life should be. It's your life.

THE CRISIS MANAGEMENT LOG

For the most part, crisis management is when the deadline has sneaked up behind you and robbed you of all choice. If you find yourself suffering from frequent crises, your problem probably has less to do with your day-to-day responsibilities and more to do with a lack of anticipation because most of the things that put us into crisis management are things that are capable of being anticipated.

The following is a good exercise to help reduce crisis management. For the next two weeks, run a crisis management log. Nothing fancy about it at all. Simply take a pad of paper and title it "Crisis Management Log" and create two columns, one for "Date" and another for "Remarks."

CRISIS MANAGEMENT LOG

Date	Remarks

For the next two weeks whenever you encounter a crisis, record it in your log. Put down the date when it occurred and a few remarks as to its detail, so that two weeks later when you go back to review the log, you will remember the particulars. After two weeks of accumulating data, go back and review every crisis you encountered during this period and ask yourself, "Which of these could have been avoided?"

Most people discover that more than 50 percent of their crises could have been avoided with better anticipation and planning. Then start the corrective steps to reduce the frequency of your crisis management events by starting deadlined items sooner or requesting needed information earlier rather than waiting until the last minute to receive it.

Some will tell me, "I work best under pressure and in crisis." If that is really true for you, work it that way. For most people, crisis management is poor time management. You are rushed, cutting corners, letting things slip through the cracks, and often having to go back and redo items. Your stress level can be elevated, affecting other things you need and want to do.

LIFE IMPROVEMENT CHART

So many people are going up the ladder of success faster, focusing on the speed and the velocity of their progress. Every once in a while, someone may come by and say to this person, "Where are you going?" and often that person shouts back, "I don't have time to think about where I'm going. I've just got to get up this ladder!"

The life improvement chart helps us to better identify

the things in our lives that we want to improve upon. It also helps us to quantify our lives now and to requantify our lives after the desired improvements are implemented. I have included a blank version and a filled-out version for you to use and follow.

Referring to the completed chart, you will notice four sections.

The first section, in the upper left, is "Rating Now." Here, you will be able to take stock of your current situation and quantify where you are. This indicates relative value. Here, you want to value each of the seven vital areas for its value to you using a scale of 1 (very little importance) to 10 (of utmost importance). Each is independent of the other. They can all be 1s, 10s, or anything else in between.

In our sample, this person has determined that his health, family, and financial areas are all 10s. His intellectual area is a 6, which means that, compared to the other three, it is only 60 percent as important. His social and professional areas are each valued at 8, which makes them more valuable than the intellectual area, but not as important as the top three. Finally, the spiritual area gets a 9. It has more value than intellectual, professional, and social but is not as important as health, family, and financial.

The 1 to 10 scale is your actual performance, your current report card. Given that an area holds a certain level of importance in your life, how are you doing in that area? In our example, this person is saying with regard to his health that, while it is worth a 10 to him as a vital area in his life, his performance is only a 6, or he is operating only at a 60 percent level. There is lots of room for improvement. The intellectual area commands a 6 for its value, and his performance is a 4, not even halfway there, which leaves a lot of room for improvement. The spiritual area is worth a 9 and his performance is an 8, so it doesn't need a lot of improvement.

Having completed both columns, we now multiply the two numbers in each row for each area and record the result in the third column, "Total Value." Under health, which is worth a 10 and has a performance value of 6, the result is 60. Under family, which has an importance of 10 and a performance of 5, the result is 50. When you add up the "Total Value" column, you arrive at 344 total quality points, which will become a meaningful number when we complete the rest of the chart.

The second section in the middle, "Desired Improvements," is for listing those changes you want in your life. I know perfection is an elusive goal, but at least in theory the things that will bring about a higher level of personal satisfaction are the things that would lead toward perfection. The objective here is to answer the question, "What would

	RATING NOW			DESIRED IMPROVEMENTS	ANTICIPATED RATING WITH IMPROVEMENTS		
	Relative Value	1-10 Scale	Total Value		Relative Value	1-10 Scale	Total Value
HEALTH	___	× ___	= ___		___	× ___	= ___
FAMILY	___	× ___	= ___		___	× ___	= ___
FINANCIAL	___	× ___	= ___		___	× ___	= ___
INTELLECTUAL	___	× ___	= ___		___	× ___	= ___
SOCIAL	___	× ___	= ___		___	× ___	= ___
PROFESSIONAL	___	× ___	= ___		___	× ___	= ___
SPIRITUAL	___	× ___	= ___		___	× ___	= ___
	Total Quality Points: ___				Total Quality Points: ___		

ACTION STATEMENTS TO BRING DESIRED IMPROVEMENTS

HEALTH		
FAMILY		
FINANCIAL		
INTELLECTUAL		
SOCIAL		
PROFESSIONAL		
SPIRITUAL		

	RATING NOW			DESIRED IMPROVEMENTS	ANTICIPATED RATING WITH IMPROVEMENTS		
	Relative Value	1-10 Scale	Total Value		Relative Value	1-10 Scale	Total Value
HEALTH	10 x	6 =	60	Lose 20 lbs.	10 x	10 =	100
FAMILY	10 x	5 =	50	Spend 6 hrs/week w/family	10 x	10 =	100
FINANCIAL	10 x	5 =	50	Save an extra $5,000 this year	10 x	10 =	100
INTELLECTUAL	6 x	4 =	24	Read 12 books	6 x	10 =	60
SOCIAL	8 x	6 =	48	Make 5 new contacts/month	8 x	10 =	80
PROFESSIONAL	8 x	5 =	40	Get a promotion	8 x	10 =	80
SPIRITUAL	9 x	8 =	72	Meditate or pray daily	9 x	10 =	90

Total Quality Points: 344

Total Quality Points: 610

ACTION STATEMENTS TO BRING DESIRED IMPROVEMENTS
HEALTH — Walk 1 mile daily
FAMILY — Spend Sunday afternoon with family
FINANCIAL — Create a budget
INTELLECTUAL — Read 10 pages each night before bedtime
SOCIAL — Schedule 2 social activities/week
PROFESSIONAL — Discuss promotion requirements with boss
SPIRITUAL — Go on a spiritual retreat this month

it take to make my 1 to 10 scale perfect in each area?" I know perfection is probably not attainable, but at least, in theory, what would have to change in my life to make each area a 10 in terms of actual, current performance? In our example, this person is saying, "If I can reduce my weight to 160 and exercise daily, then my health will be a 10." Under financial, "If I can increase my income 30 percent, it will be perfect." You might require a lot more space in this section than has been provided, as there may be many new things to change in each area to achieve greater happiness.

The third section, in the upper right, "Anticipated Ratings with Improvements," is to measure the anticipated ratings with improvements. In other words, once the desired improvements have been implemented, what will the level of quality be like in our lives, in a quantifiable way? Here we will repeat the same values in the "Relative Value" column as each holds its same relative level of importance, but what will change is the middle column, the 1 to 10 scale. Here, all areas will score a perfect 10 for performance (again, an ideal). Finally, multiply both numbers along the row for each area and record the result under the "Total Value" column. Under health, our sample person winds up with 100 points, under intellectual, 60 points, and so forth. Finally, add up the "Total Value" column. This person gets 610 total quality points versus 319 from the "Rating Now" section, before the improvements. In a measurable, quantifiable way, this person almost doubles the quality of his life.

The final section, at the bottom, is for the action statements to bring about desired improvements. List the specific steps necessary to bring about the desired improvements listed above, along with the deadlines for commencing action. If we do not insert a deadline, we are likely to procrastinate. This is for the specific steps necessary to achieve your goals and will be entered onto your daily to-do list on the day you think you will get to them.

Index